Clerks II

Other Books by
Kevin Smith:

Published Screenplays:
Clerks/Chasing Amy
The Mallrats Companion
Dogma
Jay and Silent Bob Strike Back

Graphic Novels:
Clerks: The Comic Books
Jay and Silent Bob: Chasing Dogma
Bluntman and Chronic
Daredevil: Guardian Devil
Green Arrow: Quiver
Green Arrow: The Sounds of Violence
Spider-Man/Black Cat: The Evil That Men Do
Tales From The Clerks

Humorous Essays:
Silent Bob Speaks

Coming Soon:
In Convenience: The View Askewniverse
from Clerks to Clerks II

by
Kevin Smith

FOR GRAPHITTI DESIGNS
Bob Chapman - publisher
Gayle Blume - staff
Gina Chapman
Taylor Jarrett

FOR VIEW ASKEW
Kevin Smith - publisher
Gail Stanley - staff
Ming Chen
Carol Hammond
Mike Cecconi

Design and Layout by
John Roshell @ Comicraft

•

CLERKS II: THE SCREENPLAY Published by Titan Books. A division of Titan Publishing Group Ltd., 144 Southwark Street, London SE1 0UP.

A CIP catalogue record for this title is available from the British Library.

Printed and bound in Canada.
First edition: September 2006
2 4 6 8 10 9 7 5 3 1

ISBN: 1 84576 407 2
ISBN-13: 9781845764074

Published by arrangement with View Askew and Graphitti Designs.

•

Did you enjoy this book? We love to hear from our readers. Please email us at: readerfeedback@titanemail.com or write to Reader Feedback at the above address.

To subscribe to our regular newsletter for up-to-the-minute news, great offers and competitions, email: titan-news@titanemail.com

www.titanbooks.com
www.graphittidesigns.com www.viewaskew.com

For Dante and Randal — the
two guys without whom I'd still
be sitting behind the register at
Quick Stop, simply dreaming
about making movies.

— Kevin

"To be great is to go on
To go on is to go far
To go far is to return."

— Taoist Proverb

1 EXT QUICK STOP - MORNING

As ever, the block of stores. The steel shutters are closed. Dante's shit-box pulls into his usual spot. DANTE emerges from the car, sunglasses in place. He shuffles through his keys, finds the master, and inserts it into the large padlock of the right window shutter. The lock snaps open, and Dante reaches down to grab the shutter handle. He rolls the shutter up, revealing the large, plate-glass window. It takes him a second or two to notice the ENORMOUS FUCKING FIRE ablaze within the store, on the other side of the glass, licking at the window, eager to emerge.

Quickly, Dante slams the shutter closed again, and takes a beat to look around. Did he really see what he just saw? Unsure, he slowly rolls the steel shutter up. Yup - the store's on fire inside. He closes the steel shutter again.

2 EXT QUICK STOP - LATER

Two fire trucks are now parked outside the burning husk of the store. A Fireman rolls up a still-wet hose as smoke drifts from the shattered front windows and dislodged door of the store. Into this subsiding chaos strolls RANDAL, who doesn't really notice the disaster until he's on top of it. He looks around, a bit underwhelmed, and spots...

Dante, sitting on the curb across the street, head in hands, staring at the OC mess, stunned. Randal enters the shot, standing beside Dante. He looks up and down the street.

RANDAL

Terrorists?

Dante slowly shakes his head "No." Randal nods, then thinks, then comes to a realization.

RANDAL

I left the coffee pot on again,
didn't I?

Dante slowly nods affirmatively, as the opening chords of the Talking Heads' "(Nothing But) Flowers" kick in.

RANDAL
SHIT! Now where am I gonna bring chicks to fuck when my Mom's home?

CREDITS - under which we lay out our new world...

3 EXT TRI-TOWN SUBURBIA - DAY

A hood-mounted, drive-by shot of the various local colors of tri-town suburbia ends with a whip-pan to Dante, driving, sunglasses in place. He's wearing a MOOBY'S uniform shirt, looking out the window at his world - the world he's about to leave behind.

4 EXT RANDAL'S HOUSE - DAY

Dante pulls up, laying on the horn. After a beat, Randal exits, carrying a paper and a Slim-Jim. He does a hood-slide across Dante's car, and jumps into the passenger seat. The car pulls out.

5 INT DANTE'S CAR - DAY

Dante drives. Randal opens his Slim-Jim.

RANDAL
So - you ready for your big last day?

DANTE
I am.

RANDAL
When do you and your ol' lady head down to Florida?

DANTE
Tomorrow morning. Her car's all packed up.

RANDAL
You gonna do anything crazy before you leave New Jersey forever?

DANTE
How long have you known me?

RANDAL
If I was you, I'd spray paint "Eat Pussy" across the side of the building, in huge letters.

DANTE
Why?

RANDAL
Let 'em know you were there, man.

DANTE
I'd rather let 'em know I wasn't an asshole.

RANDAL
Too late for that.

Dante offers Randal a scowl. Then...

DANTE
I'm really gonna miss you, man.

6 EXT TRI-TOWN AREA - DAY

More shots of the local color, intercut with the boys looking out at their surroundings.

7 EXT QUICK STOP - DAY

Dante's car pulls up across the street. The building's now a condemned, abandoned husk. There's a "KEEP OUT" sign on it.

RANDAL
I can't believe they haven't done anything with it yet.

DANTE
The Lord did something with it. He smited that Hell-hole.

RANDAL
"Hell-hole"... listen to you. You mean to tell me you don't miss it at all?

DANTE
God, no! Do you?

Randal eyes the store. He offers a non-committal shrug. Dante puts the car into drive.

DANTE
Of course not.

They pull out, leaving us holding on the former Stop.

8 EXT MOOBY'S - DAY

A few quick glamour shots of the fast food eatery that will be our setting.

Standing in the parking lot, Dante and Randal stare up at the side of the building - across which the words "EAT PUSSY" are spray-painted in huge letters.

Randal stares up at the OC letters, smiling. Dante looks at him and shakes his head.

9 INT MOOBY'S - DAY

WIDE on the restaurant, as the lights snap on.

CLOSE ON the coffee pot being turned on.

CLOSE ON eggs being poured onto a grill. Tilt up to Randal, who absently fries the eggs.

CLOSE ON breakfast sandwiches being wrapped. Tilt up to reveal Dante doing the wrapping.

CLOSE ON the clock, indicating 7:00am - opening time.

WIDE ON the restaurant, with Randal cooking in the kitchen and Dante jockeying the register.

10 EXT MOOBY'S - SAME

With the opening ritual complete, the day's about to begin.

11 OMITTED

12 EXT MOOBY'S - DAY

We're looking at a wall outside the restaurant. All is quiet. Suddenly, a VAN wipes the frame. We jump cut, and as the van clears, music kicks in, and we reveal JAY AND SILENT BOB leaning against that same wall. The shorter haired Jay starts air-boxing Silent Bob, 'til Silent Bob reaches into his coat and pulls out a Red Bull. Jay cracks it open, downs it, then crumples the can, kicks it across the street, and screams at the top of his lungs...

JAY

GET THE FUCK OUT OF HERE!

BLACK CARD: (The new and improved) Jay and Silent Bob.

Jay talks to Silent Bob.

JAY

Y'know, sometimes I wish I'd done a little more with my life, instead of hanging out in front of stores and shit. Like be an animal doctor. Why not me? I like seals and shit.

(thinks)

Or maybe an astronaut. Yeah - like be the first motherfucker to see a new galaxy, or discover a new alien life-form.

Silent Bob nods.

JAY

And fuck it.

Silent Bob reacts to this. Jay's still deep in thought.

JAY
Then people'd be like "There he goes. Homeboy fucked a martian once. Right in his stupid black hole.

Two TEENS approach them. Jay spots the potential customers.

JAY
Holy shit. Our first customers since our triumphant return. Act cool.

TEEN 1
You guys holding?

JAY
Shit, everything but coke, heroin, and your cock.

TEEN 2
What?

TEEN 1
How 'bout a nickel bag?

JAY
(singing)
Fifteen bucks, little man. Put that shit in my hand.

Teen 2 looks to Teen 1, a bit lost.

TEEN 1
He likes to sing.
(digging for money; toJay)
I haven't seen you guys in awhile. Where you been?

JAY
Me and Silent Bob finally bought a car, and we were cruising to the boardwalk when a fucking Middletown cop pulled us over for suspicion of mischief.

TEEN 1
What's that mean?

JAY
We were driving around with a deployed air-bag.

The Teens stare at Jay and Bob, confused.

JAY
Anyway, they pulled us over and found two pounds of Jamaican Lambs wool. The prosecutor wanted us to go away for a dime, but the judge gave us six months in rehab instead.

TEEN 1
Shit, rehab?

JAY
Yup, yup.

TEEN 2
How long were you in?

JAY
Six months, sir. I've got six months and two days on the wagon, as a good friend of Bill W.
(pulls out chip)
See? Just got my six month chip two days ago, before we got out.

TEEN 2
Yeah, but if you're holding all the time, aren't you gonna be tempted to get high?

JAY
Not with the power of Christ on my side, sir.

Jay nudges Silent Bob, who then holds a pocket Bible aloft.

TEEN 2
Is that the fucking Bible?

JAY
Hey, hey! That's the Holy fucking Bible, son.

TEEN 2
Sorry.

JAY
Any time I feel like I'm fiendin' for some dope, I ask God for guidance, say an "Our Father", then just open the Bible to any page, point at it, and read what it says. That's how Jesus talks to us.

TEEN 2
(to Teen 1)
What kinda song-bird, Jesus-freak dealers did you bring me to?

TEEN 1
I like 'em, man. They're funny.

TEEN 2
(eyeing Jay and Bob)
They're fucking stupid.

JAY
You should read your Bible, sirs. You'll find all types of weird shit in there. Like did you know Jesus was a Jew?

13 INT MOOBY'S - DAY

Randal types furiously at the Mooby-Net kiosk. Dante's behind the counter, trying to put together an order.

DANTE
I need two Cow-Tippers and we're almost out of hash browns.

RANDAL
Hold on.

DANTE
Now, Randal.

Randal half moves away from the terminal and half stays. He taps a few last keys and then heads for the kitchen.

DANTE
What're you writing over there, anyway? Your memoirs?

RANDAL
I'm battling this jackass at his blog's message board.

DANTE
About what?

RANDAL
About how he's got too much free time and no life.

DANTE
Says the guy who's flaming him on his website.

RANDAL
I can't help it. Guy pisses me off.

DANTE
What's the blog?

RANDAL
(while cooking)
WheelieBlog.org. It's this fuck in a wheelchair who's always preying on everyone's sympathies and writing

these long diatribes about how he'll never walk again, and how walkers should appreciate the blessings of their functioning legs.

DANTE
That "diatribe" as you call it sounds more like some poor, crippled guy pouring out his heart and feelings.

RANDAL
Oh, fuck him - trying to guilt me into walking around more because he's all gimped out. What kinda mind-fuck is that shit?
(dumping fries)
So I've been getting into it with him on his board - throwing it back in his stupid, crippy-boy face about how much I love to just sit around, and how I'd rather drive to the end of the block than walk.

DANTE
The guy's in a wheelchair!

RANDAL
Yeah - that's why I called him "Crippy-Boy."
(handing bag to customer)
Have a good one.

CUSTOMER
You fucking freak.

The horrified customer grabs her bag, yanks her husband by the ear, and drags him out of the joint.

DANTE
What's the matter with you?

RANDAL
What'd I do now?

DANTE
There's a crippled guy who found a way to reach out to a world he feels isolated from, and you've somehow found a way to take issue with him.

RANDAL
Sure, take his side.

DANTE
Have you become so embittered that now you feel the need to attack the handicapped?

RANDAL
What handicapped? The guy's in a wheelchair. It's not like he's Anne Frank or something

DANTE
Anne Frank?

RANDAL
Yeah, Anne Frank. The chick who was all...

Randal offers a particularly offensive impression of a blind, deaf, and dumb youth.

RANDAL
...until the Miracle Worker showed up and knocked some smarts into her.

DANTE
You're talking about Helen Keller.

RANDAL
No I'm not. I'm talking about Anne Frank. She was deaf, dumb, and blind.

DANTE
No she wasn't. Helen Keller was deaf, dumb, and blind.

RANDAL
Are you sure?

DANTE
Yep.

RANDAL
(thinks)
Then who the fuck's Anne Frank?

DANTE
Anne Frank was the little Jewish girl who hid from the Nazis in a secret room with her family. She wrote a diary?

RANDAL
Oh yeah...
(thinks)
Then I guess this guy is like Anne Frank - what with the diary and all.

DANTE
No, he's like Helen Keller, with the handicap, ya' jerk!

Randal eyeballs Dante, kinda threateningly.

RANDAL
You always gotta be right, don't you? Ya' Nazi douchebag...

14 EXT MOOBY'S - DAY

A car pulls up, and EMMA emerges. She looks at the "Eat Pussy" tag on the building - beside which lean Jay and Silent Bob. They smile at her. Jay nods to the tag.

JAY
Oh, we totally do.

Emma offers them a "dream on" look and heads inside.

15 INT MOOBY'S - SAME

Dante's at the counter, helping someone. Emma approaches.

DANTE
That'll be $12.64.

Emma climbs atop the counter, sits her ass on the kitchen closest edge, wraps her legs around Dante, and starts making out with him. The Customer watches, a bit flabbergasted. Randal saunters over, holding the customer's order. He looks at the making out Dante and Emma, and nods to the customer.

RANDAL
Avert your eyes, ya' perv.

CUSTOMER
That's not very hygenic, is all I'm gonna tell you.

The Customer exits. Randal looks at Dante and Emma, who still make out.

RANDAL
Emma, are you like this because you have an unnaturally large clit?

Breaks kiss, shocked. She lightly hits Dante.

EMMA
You just <u>had</u> to tell him.

DANTE
It just kinda came out one day.

RANDAL
He says it's so big, it's almost like a little cock. Which says all kinds of weird things about him that I don't even wanna <u>think</u> about.

EMMA
Whatever. Not that it's any of your business, but yeah - it's kinda big.

RANDAL
D'jever think about getting an operation to scale it back or something? Make it a little more normal?

EMMA
Yeah – I should probably do that, huh? I mean, it's only responsible for paralyzing orgasms. And why would I wanna cum like a porn star when I could get circumcised instead? That's a great fucking idea, Graves.

RANDAL
(to Dante)
The mouth on this chick...

DANTE
You wouldn't want to be with a girl with an over-sized clit?

RANDAL
No. 'Cause the next stop is a guy with an under-sized dick.

16 EXT MOOBY'S - LATER

EMMA is sitting on Dante's lap, making out with him, as the pair ride a swing in the Mooby's playground. She grinds him.

EMMA
You're a little hard.

DANTE
'cause you're a little close to me.

EMMA
(pulling away slightly)
I can pull back if you want...

DANTE
Can we pull back into our own apartment in Florida again?

EMMA
Really? Goddammit, Dante. How many times are we gonna talk about this? There's no point in getting an apartment anymore. My mother's pretty much told us that they're gonna give us a house as a wedding present.

DANTE
Your parents' generosity just makes me a little uncomfortable, Em. They're gonna give us a house, your Dad's giving me one of his car washes to run. It just feels weird.

EMMA
Babe, it just feels weird because you're so used to life shitting on you all the time.

DANTE
What the fuck's that mean.

EMMA
All I'm saying is that now, suddenly, you've got a woman who loves you, a new job opportunity, and a fantastic new life to look forward to, right?
(smiles)
You gotta face it, Tiger - you hit the jackpot.

Dante smiles. They kiss. Then...

OC RANDAL

'sup.

Dante and Emma break their kiss to see Randal staring at them.

DANTE

Something wrong?

RANDAL

Nope. Just saw ya' guys talking and thought I'd join you.

EMMA

God, it must be nice to have a job with so much down-time.

RANDAL

The down-time's important. If I had to deal with all the fucking mouth-breathers non-stop without a break, I'd bury my head in the deep fryer.

Emma and Dante stare at Randal for a beat, waiting for him to move along. Instead, he just adds...

RANDAL

Balls too.

EMMA

Who's watching the counter?

RANDAL

Nobody. But that's why it rocks that this place is never busy. It means we can all hang out outside and enjoy this beautiful day.

EMMA

Do you really wanna hang around out here and watch me and my fiancé make out? Are you that much of a loser?

RANDAL
Not really. I was actually gonna ask you two to knock it off while I was out here.

EMMA
I don't understand why you can't just be happy for your best friend. He finally found a woman who loves him.

RANDAL
Like you even register as a chick to me. You might as well be a dude.

EMMA
Really?

RANDAL
Sure. You're my best friend's girlfriend. You became persona-non nookie to me the moment he started diddlin' your pooter.

EMMA
So thinking of me in terms of being a girl kinda creeps you out, does it?

RANDAL
Sweetheart, I don't think of you as a girl. I don't think of you as...

Emma pulls her top up and down quickly, flashing Randal. Randal's stopped dead in his tracks.

RANDAL
Oh, that was just wrong.

EMMA
If you don't get the fuck out of here so I can spend some quality time with my man, next I'm gonna show you my "pooter."

RANDAL
(still stuck on the tits)
Why the fuck would you wanna do something like that...

Emma unbuttons her jeans.

RANDAL
Alright, alright! I'm going!

Randal rushes off. Emma takes her seat on the swing. Dante looks at Emma, disapprovingly.

DANTE
You realize now he just thinks you're trying to get him into a three-way with us? I'm never gonna hear the end of it.

EMMA
(laughing)
See? That's why I went for you. You're funny.

DANTE
Randal's funnier.

EMMA
No he's not, he's a lloyd. Like most Jersey guys. Jersey sucks and we're surrounded by morons.

DANTE
You talk tough, but when we're crossing the state line, I bet you're gonna get all sentimental for Jersey and squirt a few tears.

EMMA
Yeah, tears of joy, maybe.
(standing to leave)
On that note, I'm gonna go.

DANTE
Whoa, whoa - you're leaving?

EMMA
Yeah, I got some errands to run, and I wanna get waxed before we head out. My bush is so out of control, pretty soon, you won't even be able to see my clit.

DANTE
Please - your clit can be seen from space.

Emma laughs. She kisses Dante and gets ready to leave.

EMMA
Florida forever?

DANTE
Jersey never.

EMMA
That's better. I love you.

DANTE
Love you, too.

Emma heads off. Dante watches her go. Randal re-joins Dante outside. They watch Emma pull out. Then...

RANDAL
Dude, I'm pretty sure your lady wants to get me and you together in a three-way.

17 EXT MOOBY'S - DAY

A station wagon pulls up, packed with a mother, father and son, whistling happily. A somewhat dweeby, maybe borderline retarded ELIAS emerges, dressed in a Mooby's uniform. He goes around to the driver's side and kisses the driver, his MOTHER, goodbye. As she pulls away, he heads into the restaurant.

18 INT MOOBY'S - SAME

As Elias enters, still whistling, Randal's standing there, eyeballing him.

RANDAL
Dude, how old are you?

ELIAS
You know I'm nineteen, Randal. You wouldn't work for me last week, remember? 'cause you said working on my birthday'd help me build character.

Elias notices the "Funployee of the Month" picture - his - with a Randal-added word balloon that reads "I eat cock." He takes the word balloon down, crumpling it up.

ELIAS
At least you spelled "cock" right this time.

RANDAL
Why the fuck are you still getting rides from your mother? And even worse, what the fuck are you kissing her goodbye for? What is she, your fucking prom date?

Randal replaces the removed word balloon with a drawing of a cock, exploding with a fireworks-display-like helping of cum.

ELIAS
You're not gonna bother me today, Randal. I'm in too good a mood.

RANDAL
Because your mom slipped you the tongue?

ELIAS
No. Because I just read online that there's gonna be a live-action "Transformers" movie.

RANDAL
And?

ELIAS
And as you know, my online handle is Optimus Prime, so not only is it awesome that there's gonna be a live-action "Transformers", but I'm positioned with the best possible 'net handle and email address for when the movie comes out.

RANDAL
Oh, you're gonna be rolling in the pussy, man.

ELIAS
Don't be gross.

RANDAL
Says the guy who was just playing tonsil-hockey with his mother.

ELIAS
(calling out)
MISTER DANTE!

Dante swings open the bathroom door, where he's taking his morning dump, reading a paper.

DANTE
(as if said a thousand times)
Leave Elias alone, Randal.

That's when Dante notices the family sitting across from the open bathroom door, staring at him, aghast. The Father covers his kids' eyes.

FATHER
Don't look at his wee-wee!

Dante quickly closes the bathroom door.

Elias smiles smugly at Randal as he pulls on the drive-thru headphones. Randal shakes his head.

RANDAL
Dude, the Transfomers sucked.

ELIAS
Oh - no they didn't! They were more than meets the eye! They could beat the pants off Ranger Danger any day.

RANDAL
Sh'yeah - I'll lose sleep wondering whether you're right about that or not. I thought you weren't even allowed to watch a lot of TV in your house because you're all Christian and shit.

ELIAS
As it turns out, cars and trucks that turn into robots aren't blasphemous. 'cause, my Pastor says machines can turn into other machines, and it's not a slight against God.

RANDAL
The "Transformers" were a total slight against God, inasmuch as God sent His only begotten Son to die on the cross to redeem mankind, and all we did to pay Him back was make terrible fucking cartoons like the "Transformers."

ELIAS
Well, at Bible Camp, we did this flow chart that kind of proved, or whatever, that since God created man, and man created the "Transformers"... then the "Transformers" are like a gift from God, Randal.

RANDAL
No, sir. They're not from God. They're an unholy curse from the Beast Who Is Called the Desolate One!

ELIAS
(covering his ears)
I don't wanna hear this, Randal...

RANDAL
(taunting him)
The First of the Fallen, the Spoiler of Virgins, the Master of Abortions!

ELIAS
(backing up toward the drive-thru window)
You know I don't like to talk about dark forces, Randal.

RANDAL
(singing King Diamond)
Let me help you... out of the chair! G...G...Grandma!

Just then, Jay and Silent Bob pop up in the drive-thru window, chiming in with the song.

JAY
Grandma, what was it like?! To be on that Holiday site!

As Jay climbs through the window into the restaurant, Randal switches gears, singing The Invisible Guests instead.

RANDAL
Late that... night I... awoke from my...

JAY
(joining in, moshing Elias with Randal)
sleep hearing... unknown...voices...

JAY AND RANDAL
(together; high pitched)
...LAUGHING INSANE!!!

Elias runs off, screaming, forgetting that he's still wearing the connected drive-thru headphones. He gets a few feet then is suddenly yanked backwards, landing on the floor. Randal, Jay and Silent Bob stare at him as he lays there, groaning.

19 INT MOOBY'S - DAY

Dante cleans the front windows. Through the window, we see BECKY pull up and get out of her car outside. Dante waves to her and she waves back, collecting her purse. Randal rockets up to Dante.

RANDAL
Oh, what the fuck was that?

DANTE
What?

RANDAL
That wave?

DANTE
I saw Becky, so I waved.

RANDAL
She'll be in here in twenty seconds.

DANTE
And?

RANDAL
And you've gotta greet her before she gets inside, ya' fucking ass kiss? What's that all about?

DANTE
It's called friendship.

RANDAL
She's your boss. You can't be friends with your boss.

DANTE
No - you can't be friends with your boss. I like my boss.

RANDAL
(eyeing Dante)
I think there's something going on between you two.

DANTE
You're crazy.

RANDAL
You spend an awful lot of time talking to her.

DANTE
I spend an awful lot of time talking to you, too.

RANDAL
And I've always maintained you're harboring an unrequited homosexual crush on me.

DANTE
We're just friends.

RANDAL
That's what I keep telling you.

DANTE
No, you idiot. Me and Becks.

RANDAL
"Becks"? I knew it! You're fucking around with the boss!

DANTE
Yeah - that's why I'm moving to Florida with my fiancé.

RANDAL
Why would you wanna fuck around with someone your own age, man? If you wanted to sow some of your wild oats, there are all these fine, young chicks who stop in here after school.

DANTE
First off, I'm not cheating on my fiancé. Secondly, if I was gonna cheat on my fiancé, it wouldn't be with a teenager.

RANDAL
Why not? The best part of this job is all the barely legal pussy that comes in. And they all look up to me because I've got a driver's license. It's awesome.

DANTE
You're thirty three!

RANDAL
You show me one thirty three year old chick who's as buck-wild in bed as her seventeen year old counterpart? Seventeen year olds nowadays are crazy, man. They're up for anything. They even like it when you go ass-to-mouth.

Dante is stunned and disgusted.

DANTE
Oh... my... God...

RANDAL
What?

DANTE
Are you serious?

RANDAL
I don't fuck around when it comes to ass-to-mouth.

DANTE
YOU NEVER GO ASS-TO-MOUTH!

RANDAL
It's never my idea. These young chicks today get all horned-up, and they tell you to go ass-to-mouth.

DANTE
YOU NEVER GO ASS-TO-MOUTH, RANDAL!

RANDAL
You sound like my mom.

Becky enters. She's dressed in a managerial variation of the standard Mooby uniform.

RANDAL
Becks, do you ever go ass-to-mouth?

BECKY
You never go ass-to-mouth.

RANDAL
You've never gone ass-to-mouth?

DANTE
YOU NEVER GO ASS-TO-MOUTH!

BECKY
I've never gone ass-to-mouth.

RANDAL
Not even once?

BECKY
Not even ever.

RANDAL
You're both so repressed.
(to Becky)
Alright, look - you've given a blowjob, right?

BECKY
(flabbergasted)
I haven't even put my purse down yet...

RANDAL
That's a yes.
(to Dante)
And I know you've gone down on chicks.

BECKY
What's your point?

RANDAL
Well, when you're done chowing down on the no-no parts of your lover, you kiss 'em, right? That's just like going ass-to-mouth.

BECKY
Okay, I'm pretty sure you just compared a vagina to an asshole.

RANDAL
And?

BECKY
Have you re-stocked all the napkin holders yet?

RANDAL
That's an Elias job.

BECKY
That comparison of pink and brown eyes just made it a Randal job.

ELIAS
(from OC)
Zing!

RANDAL
(to OC)
Shut the fuck up, Go-Bot.
(to Becky)
I could probably sue this whole corporation for sexual harassment. You're just making me re-stock the napkin holders because of my firmly held beliefs on the subject of ass-to-mouth.

DANTE
YOU NEVER GO ASS-TO-MOUTH!

RANDAL
(to Dante)
Would you grow up?

He heads off. Becky and Dante watch him go.

BECKY
I'm gonna tell you this because we're friends...
(quietly)
But sometimes, in the heat of the moment, it's forgivable to go ass-to-mouth.

OC RANDAL
I KNEW IT!

Becky shakes her head and enters the kitchen, leaving the stunned Dante standing there, mouth agape.

20 EXT MOOBY'S - DAY

Jay and Silent Bob ride their wall. After a beat, Jay says to Silent Bob...

JAY
I'm fucking bored, man. And boredom's the first step on the road to relapse.

Silent Bob studies Jay for a beat, then exits the frame. He comes back with a boom box, sets it down and presses play. Q Lazsurus' "Goodbye Horses" begins playing (that's the song from "Silence of the Lambs" that Buffalo Bill dances and tucks to). Jay starts doing his best Buffalo Bill dance, pulling out Chapstick and applying it like lipstick.

JAY
Would you fuck me? I'd fuck me. I'd fuck me hard...

21 INT BACK OFFICE - DAY 21

Becky's at her desk, looking at un-Mooby looking, medical paperwork. She's a bit stressed about what she's reading.

BECKY
Shit...

There's a knock at the door, and Dante enters. Becky shoves the paperwork in her purse and smiles up at him.

DANTE
Well hello Ms. Scott.

BECKY
Well here he is - the Escape Artist.

DANTE
I'm not gone yet.

BECKY
Please. You've been gone for the last month. When do you guys leave?

DANTE
We start driving tomorrow morning. I left you the forwarding address for my last check on the calendar.

BECKY
(looks at desk calendar)
So you did. That's her parents' house, right?

DANTE
Yes - but we're only there 'til the wedding. Then, from what I hear, her parents are giving us a house.

BECKY
Niiiiiice. So I guess dowries are making a comeback.

DANTE
Her Dad sweetened the pot with two fatted calves and a goat.

BECKY
(laughs)
I'm gonna miss you, Hicks.

DANTE
I'm gonna miss you, too.

BECKY
I still can't believe you're just gonna leave me alone in this place. With Randal Graves of all people.

DANTE
Quit. Move to Florida. You can work at the car wash with me.

BECKY
Wow. You make it sound so tempting. How can I say no? Oh yeah: 'cause it's a fucking car wash in Florida.

DANTE
Like it's any worse than this place?

BECKY
Hurl the insults all you want, Buddy-Man. As soon as my uncle's back on his feet, it's not like I'm staying here.

DANTE
How's he doing?

BECKY
Alot better. It only took two years and a shit-load of chemo, but his red cell count's almost back to normal.

DANTE
That's great.

BECKY
Yeah, great for me, too. A couple weeks in this crap-shack turned into a couple years a little too quickly. But, Hicks - we can sit here, making small talk about your last day and what I'm gonna do once your gone, or we can treat this like any other work day.

Becky reaches into her desk drawer and extracts some nail polish. She holds it up and smiles at Dante.

22 INT MOOBY'S - DAY

Elias plays with an order, from which he pulls an onion ring. Randal stocks a napkin holder.

ELIAS
Randal.

Randal looks up. Elias extends the onion ring toward him.

ELIAS
(in trailer voice)
"One ring to rule them all..."

RANDAL
And you wonder why no chick'll ever let you stick your cock in her.

ELIAS
I never wondered that.

RANDAL
S'yeah, because you've accepted the fact that you'll never get a chick a long time ago.

ELIAS
I could get a chick if I wanted.

RANDAL
Who're you kidding? You can't get a chick, ya' mook. You're too weird and sad.

ELIAS
I turn down chicks left and right.

RANDAL
(nodding to Elias' hands)
Your chicks are your left and right.

ELIAS
Sh'yeah, right. What do you know?

RANDAL
Uh, I know you're a huge fucking nerd of Potsie-like proportions, and no chicks dig nerds. Especially nerds who dig "Lord of the Rings."

ELIAS
(defensively)
Chicks dig "Lord of the Rings", Randal.

RANDAL
Yeah - the kind of chicks who're into swords and elves and shit. And I wouldn't fuck them with the Torch of Gondor.

ELIAS
Ewww, you're so gross.

A CUSTOMER enters and approaches the counter. Elias puts on his customer service hat.

ELIAS
Welcome to Mooby's, may I take your order?

CUSTOMER
I'll have an Udder-ly Delicious Moo ilk shake, a Skinny Calf, and an order of onion rings, please.

Elias punches the order into the register, quietly adding...

ELIAS
"One ring to rule them all..."

CUSTOMER
"One ring to find them..."

RANDAL
Oh, Jesus...

ELIAS
"One ring to bring them all..."

CUSTOMER
"And in the darkness, bind them!"

Elias and the Customer hold up "Ring" replicas to one another and high five. Randal shakes his head, disgusted.

ELIAS
YES! How many times?

CUSTOMER
Three for "Fellowship", two for "Towers", and four for "Return."

ELIAS
(pointing to himself)
Five for "Return."

RANDAL
(getting pissed)
Alright, look - there's only one "Return", okay! And it ain't of a King, it's of the Jedi!

CUSTOMER
(to Elias, off Randal)
"Star Wars" geek.

RANDAL
Oh, I'm the geek? Look at you two - whipping out your Precious-es.

ELIAS
(off Randal)
You'll have to excuse him. He's not down with the Trilogy.

RANDAL
What the fuck happened to this world? There's only one Trilogy, you fuckin' morons.

CUSTOMER
Maybe we should start calling your friend Padme because he loves Mannequin Skywalker so much.
(doing the robot)
"Danger! Danger! My name is Anakin! My shitty acting is ruining saga!

ELIAS
(to Randal)
You're crazy, Jar-Jar!

RANDAL

Oh, I'm crazy? Those fucking Hobbit movies were boring as hell. All it was was a bunch of people walking. Three movies of people walking to a fucking volcano. Here's the first movie...

With feigned purpose, Randal walks a few feet, looking to some imaginary Mount Doom in the distance.

RANDAL

Here's the second movie...

He does it again, though he suddenly stops and side-steps, as if something has fallen next to him. Then, he continues his walk cycle anew.

CUSTOMER

He is waaay off. Loser.

RANDAL

Are you ready for the third one...

Randal walks again, then stops and pull an imaginary ring off his finger, tossing it into the imaginary lava. He shrugs, turns, and walks again, in the opposite direction.

A pair of diners who've been watching this display chime in from the sidelines.

DINER

Fucking a.

RANDAL

Even the fucking trees walked in those movies.

CUSTOMER

Alright, I've had enough of you. Your simplistic analysis of the Trilogy aside, "The Lord of the Rings" was a massive achievement that even the Academy recognized when they gave Peter Jackson the best directing Oscar - an award your little friend George "Toy-Boy" Lucas has never, and will never, win.

ELIAS
Ooo - sick burn.

RANDAL
Lemme tell ya' something - if Peter Jackson really wanted to blow me away, he would've ended that last "Rings" picture at the logical closure point - not the twenty five endings that followed.

ELIAS
And what's the logical closure point?

CUSTOMER
Yeah, friend - enlighten us.

RANDAL
When Frodo wakes up from his coma or whatever, and the little Hobbits are jumping up and down on his bed, and then, Sam leans in the doorway, and gives Frodo that very fucking gay look.

ELIAS
Not the "Rings" Randal! Say what you will about Jesus, but leave the "Rings" out of this!

CUSTOMER
I'm gonna kick your fucking ass back to the shire if you don't shut your fucking mouth!

RANDAL
That look was so gay, I thought Sam was gonna tell the l'il Hobbits to take a walk, so he could saunter over to Frodo and suck his fucking cock. Now that would've been an Academy Award-worthy ending.

CUSTOMER
Hey! Faggot! They're not gay! They're Hobbits!

RANDAL
And then, after the Sam/Frodo suck fest, right before the credits roll... Sam fucking flat-out bricks in Frodo's mouth.

Completely distressed, the Customer suddenly vomits.

23 INT BACK OFFICE - SAME

The laughing Randal suddenly bursts into the office, where Dante paints Becky's toe-nails. She quickly puts her feet down and Dante hides the nail polish.

RANDAL
I made fun of "Lord of the Rings" so hard, it made some super-geek puke all over the counter. Where do we keep the mop and bucket so Elias can clean it up?

DANTE
In the closet with the rest of the cleaning products.

RANDAL
We have cleaning products?

Randal closes the door, leaving Becky and Dante. He then re opens the door, looking at them suspiciously.

RANDAL
What smells in here?

BECKY
Bye.

Randal eyeballs Becky, then turns his glare on Dante.

RANDAL
(quietly; menacingly)
I'm on to you...

Dante reacts as Randal slowly closes the door, nodding at him.

BECKY
You know he's not gonna make it here long once you're not around to protect him anymore, don'tcha?

DANTE
(goes back to nail painting)
You're the one encouraging him, out there advocating ass-to-mouth.

BECKY
I wasn't advocating it, ya' big prude. I said it was fine once in awhile. Like you wouldn't do it if Emma told you to?

DANTE
Christ, no.

BECKY
I thought love knew no bounds.
(stops)
Ew. That came off kinda catty, didn't it?

DANTE
A little daytime soap-ish, yeah.

BECKY
I'm sorry. I don't know why I said that. I actually kinda like Emma.

DANTE
Me too.

BECKY
So that's why you're getting married...

DANTE
I can't wait 'til you get engaged one day, so I can bust your balls as hard as you've busted mine.

BECKY
You're gonna be waiting a long time, sir.

DANTE
Oh that's right, I forgot: you're the cold-hearted ice princess that doesn't believe in marriage.

BECKY
I'm not saying it's not right for you, but, yes - I feel marriage goes against our primal nature.

DANTE
To be loved?

BECKY
To fuck as much as possible, spread the seed around, and keep the species going. And all that shit they feed us in the movies and greeting cards is just propaganda to get us to marry, have kids, and keep the economy going. Marriage is just the keystone to economics.

DANTE
You're such a sappy girl. You trying to tell me you don't believe in love, Beckala?

BECKY
In romantic love? No. Like, I love my parents. I love my car. I love you. But romantic love? Hearts and flowers? "There's only one person for me,"? C'mon. You know how many people are out there? Odds are there's always gonna be someone who's a better match for you than the person you end up marrying.

DANTE
So, based on your theory, there's someone out there who's better for me than Emma?

BECKY
Oh no - I'm not touching that one.

DANTE
Wait a second - you don't think I really love her?

BECKY
(thinks)
I think you love what she represents.

DANTE
Which is?

BECKY
C'mon, Dante - she was the girl who wouldn't give you the time of day back in high school. And years later, after she's played the field and realized how unsatisfying the so-called "hotties" are, she went for someone who looks...

DANTE
Oh my God, you're gonna say "fugly", aren't you?

BECKY
Unconventional.

DANTE
Nice back-pedal.

BECKY
Thank you. It took her a few years to figure out that shit every little girl's Mother tries to teach her, but she has to learn herself. And that's that that guys that look like you have a lot more to offer, because you'll always try harder than a pretty boy.

DANTE
What am I, some hideous fucking C.H.U.D. over here?

BECKY
No - you're a catch.
(quickly adds)
Kinda. And Emma's a catch, too. Because not only is she pretty, but she'll make all your decisions for you. Which is lucky, because you're pretty terrible at making decisions

DANTE
So my last day is all about you telling me what an ugly, indecisive loser I am.

BECKY
(chuckling)
C'mon, Dante - you worked at Quick Stop for, like, a decade. And you've been here for almost a year now? And since day one at both

jobs, all you talked about was getting out so you could "start your life." But it wasn't until Emma walked in here and was like "Move down to Florida with me, and I'll fuck your brains out, and my Daddy'll give you a job," 'til you did something about it. And I mean, I get it: Emma's your golden ticket.

DANTE
So what's that make you?

BECKY
I'm just the girl who fucks ugly, indecisive losers in the kitchen once this place is closed.

The pair crack up. There's a long beat of silence in which the two eyeball one another, smiling. Then...

DANTE
We're never gonna talk about it, are we?

BECKY
What is there to say?

DANTE
Do you regret it?

BECKY
Do you?

DANTE
(thinks)
I only regret it was on the prep station table.

BECKY
S'yeah - you regret it? You weren't the one who got mayo in your cootch.

They laugh, followed by a long beat during which they look at one another.

BECKY
What do you want me to say? We were drunk. It just kinda happened.
(pokes his nose)
You're just lucky I'm not one of those monogamists like your girlfriend. Or else I might try to make you to stay in Jersey.

DANTE
If anyone could do it, it'd be you.

Becky looks at him, really touched. Both want to say something. Suddenly, Randal enters again, and both look up, trying not to look "caught". Randal eyes them, then...

RANDAL
Your ol' lady's out there, looking for you.

Randal slowly closes the door. Dante closes the nail polish and excuses himself. Becky watches him go.

24 INT MOOBY'S - SAME

Dante emerges from the kitchen to see Emma hopping excitedly. She rushes forward and grabs Dante's arm.

EMMA
Come outside! I've got a surprise for you!

Emma leads Dante out the door.

25 EXT MOOBY'S - SAME

Silent Bob smokes as Jay (pants and boxers down around his ankles, dick tucked back) does the full Buffalo Bill. Dante and Emma emerge.

DANTE
This is my surprise?

EMMA
No...

Emma drags Dante OC, as Jay continues his performance.

JAY
(singing)
Goodbye, horses! I'm flying over you!

26 INT MOOBY'S - SAME

Randal's at the Mooby internet terminal, typing away. Elias saunters up, joining him.

ELIAS
Hey!

Randal doesn't react or engage him in return.

ELIAS
Oh. So... are you looking for a good Transformers site? Because at carstobots.com, you can create an avatar that's your picture morphed to look like a robot.

RANDAL
(not looking up)
C'mon, man - you know I only surf Transformers sites when there're girls around, so they could see how cool I am.

ELIAS
So what're you doing then?

RANDAL
I'm trying to secure a going away present for Mr. Dante.

ELIAS
Really? Well how about an Arwen sword replica?

RANDAL
(with disdain)
What?!

ELIAS
(suddenly scared)
Oh. I just... 'cause it's thoughtful and practical.

RANDAL
I was thinking of something a little more sexy.

ELIAS
What's sexier than an Elf princess' sword?

RANDAL
A donkey show.

ELIAS
What's that?

RANDAL
You ever seen a chick give a mule a blowjob?

ELIAS
(horrified)
EWWW, NO!

RANDAL
(covering his mouth)
Shhhhh! If you spoil this, I'm gonna brain you. Are you gonna keep your mouth shut?

Elias half-nods. Randal removes his hand.

ELIAS
That's bestiality, Randal.

RANDAL
(back to typing)
At its finest, I hope.

ELIAS
Who would wanna see something like that?

RANDAL
Me. Dante. You.

ELIAS
I don't wanna see something like that. Why would you wanna see something like that?

RANDAL
Because it's fucked up. And I wanna see if a chick with a mouth fulla donkey spunk swallows.
(reading screen)
"Kinky Kelly and the Sexy Stud. Fresh from their dirty debut in Tijuana, Kelly's taking it on the road. Taking it in the ass, that is."
(admiringly)
You've gotta give it up for Oscar Wilde-like wordplay that good.

ELIAS
(looking away from the screen)
Do they show pictures?

RANDAL
Just one of Kinky Kelly sucking off Optimus Prime.

ELIAS
Really?!

Elias scurries to see the non-existent image, and Randal lightly slaps him in the head, as if to say "You idiot."

RANDAL
Lemme borrow your cell phone.

ELIAS
I'm only supposed to use it to call my parents, in case of an emergency.

RANDAL
This is an emergency. We've gotta lock up Kinky Kelly for tonight so we can give Mr. Dante a memorable send-off. You love Mr. Dante, don'tcha?

ELIAS
In a non-gay way.

RANDAL
Well then gimme your phone. Because Mr. Dante's never seen a donkey show, and it'd be nice to give him this before he goes off to Florida to get married and do all those other things that prevent a guy from ever seeing a fucked up donkey show in his lifetime.

Elias hands Randal his cell. Randal dials.

RANDAL
(into phone)
Yeah, hi. I was hoping to schedule Kinky Kelly for a performance... Tonight?... 'kay.
(covers phone)
I'm on hold. Fingers crossed.

Elias crosses his fingers.

RANDAL
We should cross dicks, too.

Elias absently reaches for his pants. Randal stops him.

RANDAL
No.

27 EXT MOOBY'S PARKING LOT - DAY

Emma's sitting cross-legged on the back of her car, a box of envelopes in front of her. Dante's beside her. We're moving toward them in a POV that Becky steps into.

BECKY
Work, work, work - that's all you ever think about, Hicks.

EMMA
Hey, Becks.

BECKY
Hey, Emma. Great shirt.

EMMA
Isn't it? I love it. But what I love even more, are these.
(hands Becky an envelope)
These came in early, and I just had to come back and show Dante. And give you yours, of course. And I have one for Randal, I guess.

BECKY
What is it?

She opens it to see a wedding invitation.

EMMA
I know it's three months away, but we'd love it if you could make the trip down.

BECKY
Um... yeah. I wouldn't miss it.

DANTE
I thought we were gonna wait 'til we got down there to pick a date.

EMMA
Awwww... Him's thinking again. That is so cute!

Emma pets Dante's head a bit condescendingly. Becky looks really uncomfortable with the whole scene.

EMMA
If we left anything up to these jackals, nothing would ever get done, would it?

Emma kisses Dante, and then hugs him in such a way that Becky and Dante can lock eyes.

BECKY
I guess you've just gotta make their decisions for 'em sometimes.

Dante's look to Becky as she leaves, giving us the impression, for the first time, that the guy might feel a bit trapped.

28 INT MOOBY'S - SAME

Randal's on Elias' cell. Elias listens to the convo.

RANDAL
Alright, then I'll see you 'round nine?... Got it. Thanks.

Randal hangs up and tosses Elias his cell phone.

RANDAL
My friend, tonight, we bring a bit of TJ to the Jersey 'burbs.

ELIAS
I don't know about this, Randal. 'cause how do we know this isn't a hoax? Like, were there any pictures on the website?

RANDAL
Strangely, no. But if you've seen pics of one chick sucking off a donkey, you've seen 'em all.

ELIAS
What if you haven't ever seen pictures of anything like that?

RANDAL
Then you must be as blind as Anne Frank. Because what's the use in having an internet connection if you're not using it to look at weird, fucked up pictures of dirty sex you'll never have yourself?

Elias absently nods, heading into the kitchen. Randal eyes him for a beat. Then catches on, following Elias.

RANDAL
Holy shit. I never pieced it together 'til right now. You're a virgin, aren't you?

ELIAS
You know I have a girlfriend, Randal.

RANDAL
Oh yeah. What's her name again?

ELIAS
Myra Hodgkiss.

RANDAL
You made that up, didn't you? That name sounds so made up.

ELIAS

No.

RANDAL

Seriously, Elias. Have you and Myra had sex yet?

ELIAS

That's just kind of personal, Randal.

RANDAL

C'mon, man. I tell you about my sex life all the time. I let you smell my fingers after I fucked Hayden Weathers' kid sister in the office that one time, didn't I?

ELIAS

You kinda made me smell your fingers.

RANDAL

Well maybe you just don't like the pussy. Maybe you're all about the cock.

ELIAS

No, I like the pussy.

RANDAL

So did Myra ever give you a crack at her crack or what?

ELIAS

Not that it's any of your business, Randal, but she can't.

RANDAL

Why?

Elias looks at Randal like he should know.

RANDAL
Elias, C'mon! You've gotta start trusting me more. Because once Dante's gone, you're gonna be my new best friend.

ELIAS
(incredulous but hopeful)
No I'm not.

RANDAL
Who else am I gonna hang out with? It's gonna be you and me, buddy. So you've gotta learn to start trusting me. Open up and tell me shit. Like why haven't you fucked Myra yet?

Elias tries to weigh the seriousness of Randal's words. He then relents, looks around, and quietly says to Randal.

ELIAS
We can't because of Pillow-Pants.

RANDAL
What the fuck's Pillow-Pants?

ELIAS
Pillow-Pants is the little troll who lives in her pussy.

Randal stares at Elias, perplexed. Elias is frustrated by Randal's lack of understanding.

ELIAS
Pillow-Pants is her pussy-troll, duh.

Randal's dumbfounded.

ELIAS
You know how every girl's parents put a pussy-troll in them when the girls are young to keep them from having pre-marital sex?

At a loss, Randal offers a half-nod to the deluded Elias.

ELIAS
Well Myra's is named Pillow-Pants. And even though she wants to have sex with me, she says if I put my thing in her, Pillow-Pants will bite it off. So I've gotta wait 'til Pillow-Pants gets peed out of her body on Myra's twenty first birthday before we can have sex.

RANDAL
(long beat)
And Myra told you this?

ELIAS
Boyfriends and girlfriends talk to each other about sex stuff, Randal. You'd know this if you ever had a girlfriend.

RANDAL
Have you and Myra ever even kissed yet?

ELIAS
We would've already, if it wasn't for Lister-Fiend.

RANDAL
(thinks; then)
Lister-Fiend is the Mouth-Troll, isn't he?

ELIAS
(shaking his head)
Women...

Randal stares at Elias for a long beat. Then...

RANDAL
I'll be right back.

Randal rushes from behind the counter over to Dante who's manning a register, waiting on a customer.

RANDAL
You're never gonna believe what Elias just told me...

DANTE
(off customer)
Look who it is, Randal.

Randal looks at the smiling, arrogant-looking customer and deflates slightly.

LANCE
Randal Graves. You work here too? Jesus - anyone else from our graduating class back there?

Randal and Dante stare at Lance dead-eyed. This is the nightmare: having to serve an old classmate.

RANDAL
Well, well, well. Pickle-Fucker.

LANCE
Man, look at you two "Funployees". Nothing's changed. You know I'll bet dollars to donuts that when you're not fighting over who short first - Han or Greedo - you can still muster up enough energy to make fun of other people.

RANDAL
Yeah. So hurry up and order so you can get out of here, and we can make fun of you.

LANCE
Oh, I don't know if you're in a position to make fun of anyone anymore, Graves. Thirty two and

you're flipping burgers? I'd heard before that, it was the Quick Stop - for like ten years.

RANDAL

We can't all be internet millionaires.

ELIAS

Who's an internet millionaire?

DANTE

Elias, this is Lance Dowds. We went to high school with together. A few years ago, he built a search engine that compiles the lowest prices of merchandise you can buy online. You might've heard of it: mad-ducats.com.

ELIAS

Didn't that just sell to Amazon for, like, twenty million bucks?

RANDAL

Yeah, but back before he was the mad-ducats guy, he was just Pickle Fucker.

See, Freshman year, the Seniors would hunt us down and put us through what they called "Initiation." Sometimes they'd stuff us into lockers, or push us into the girls' shower naked. But Lance here got the worst of it: the Seniors yanked his pants down and shoved a pickle up his ass and made him walk ten feet. If the pickle fell out before he hit the ten foot mark, he had to take a bite of it, re-insert it, and walk again.

ELIAS

Eww...

Mooby
family
n fun™

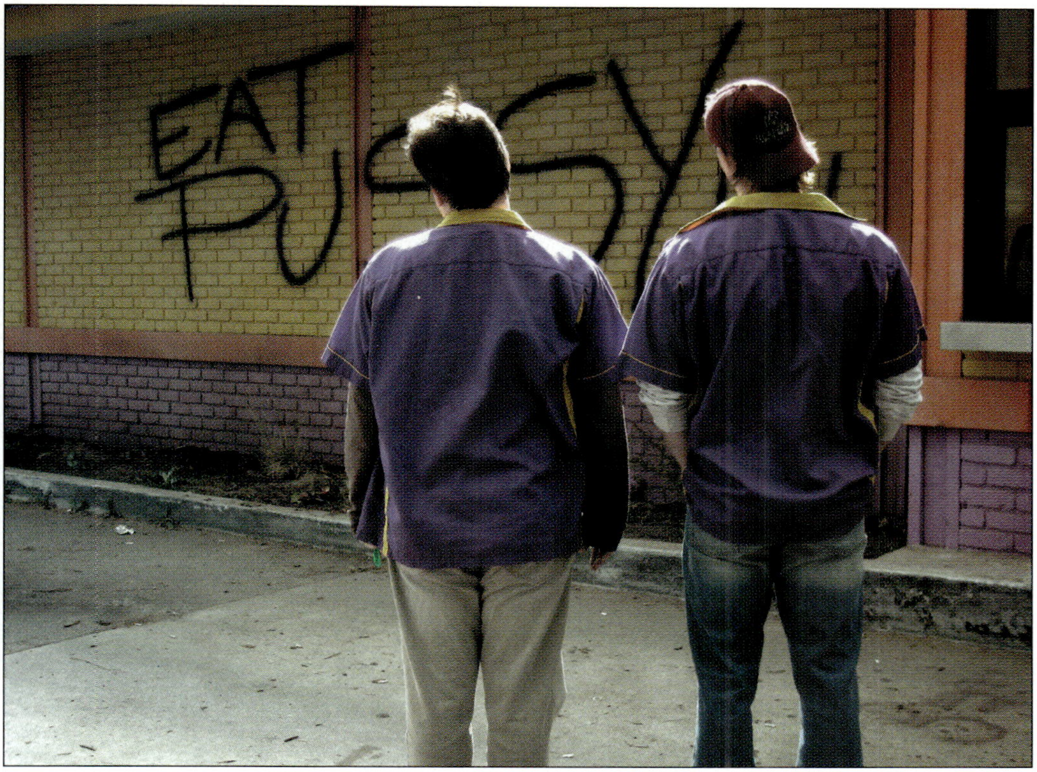
EAT
PUSSY

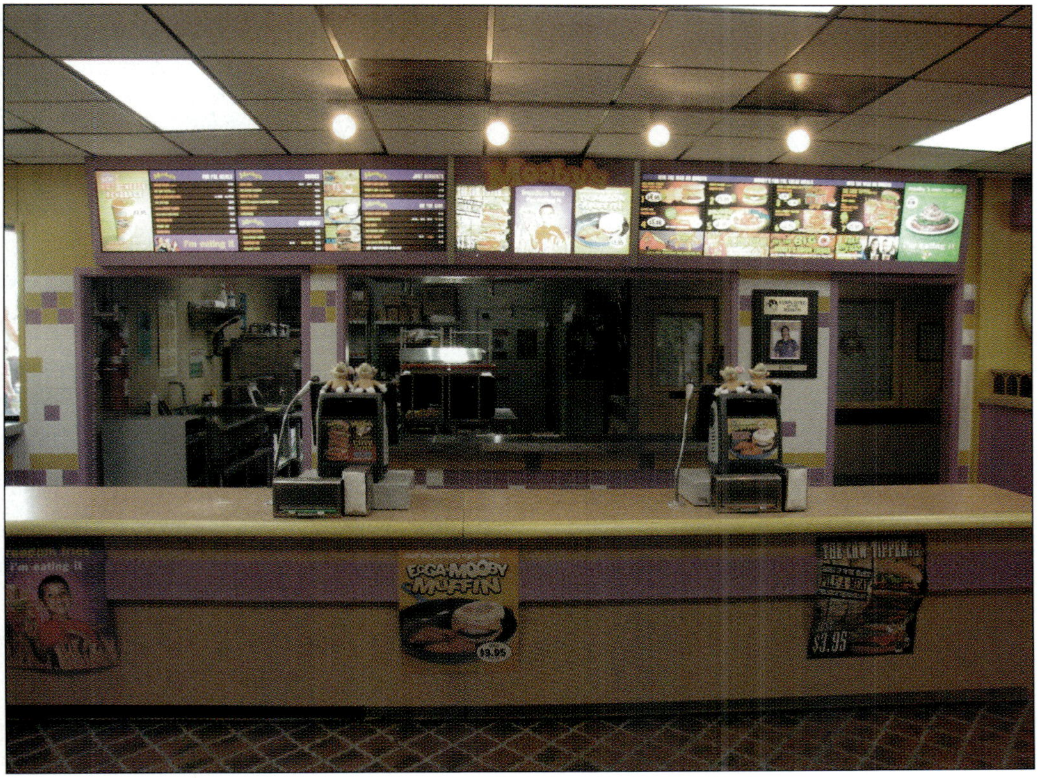
I'm eating it
EGGA-MOOBY MUFFIN
$3.95
$3.95

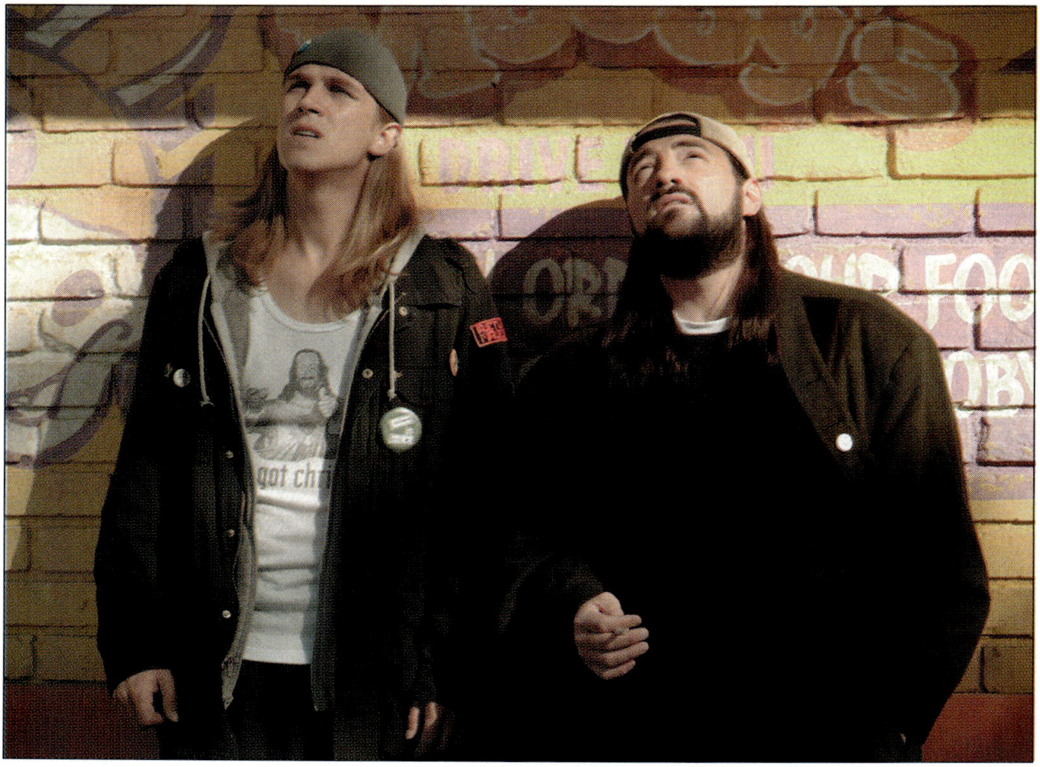

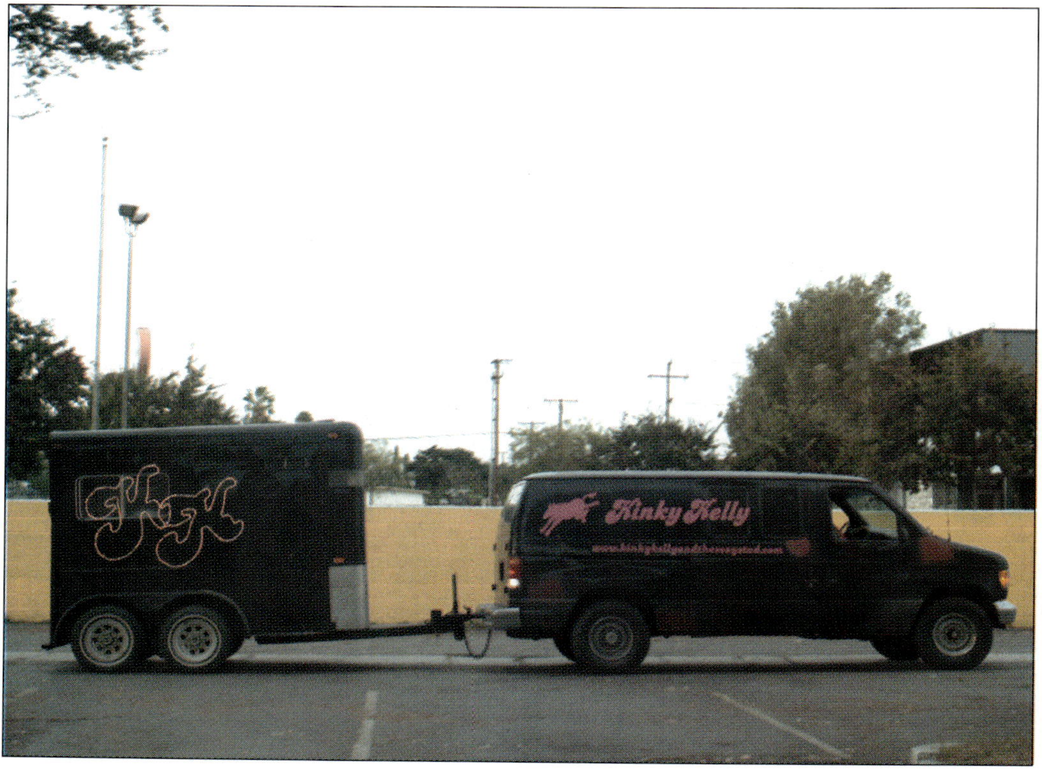

ALWAYS
OPEN.

CLERKS II

ON JULY 21ST GET READY FOR THE SECOND COMING.

www.clerks2.com

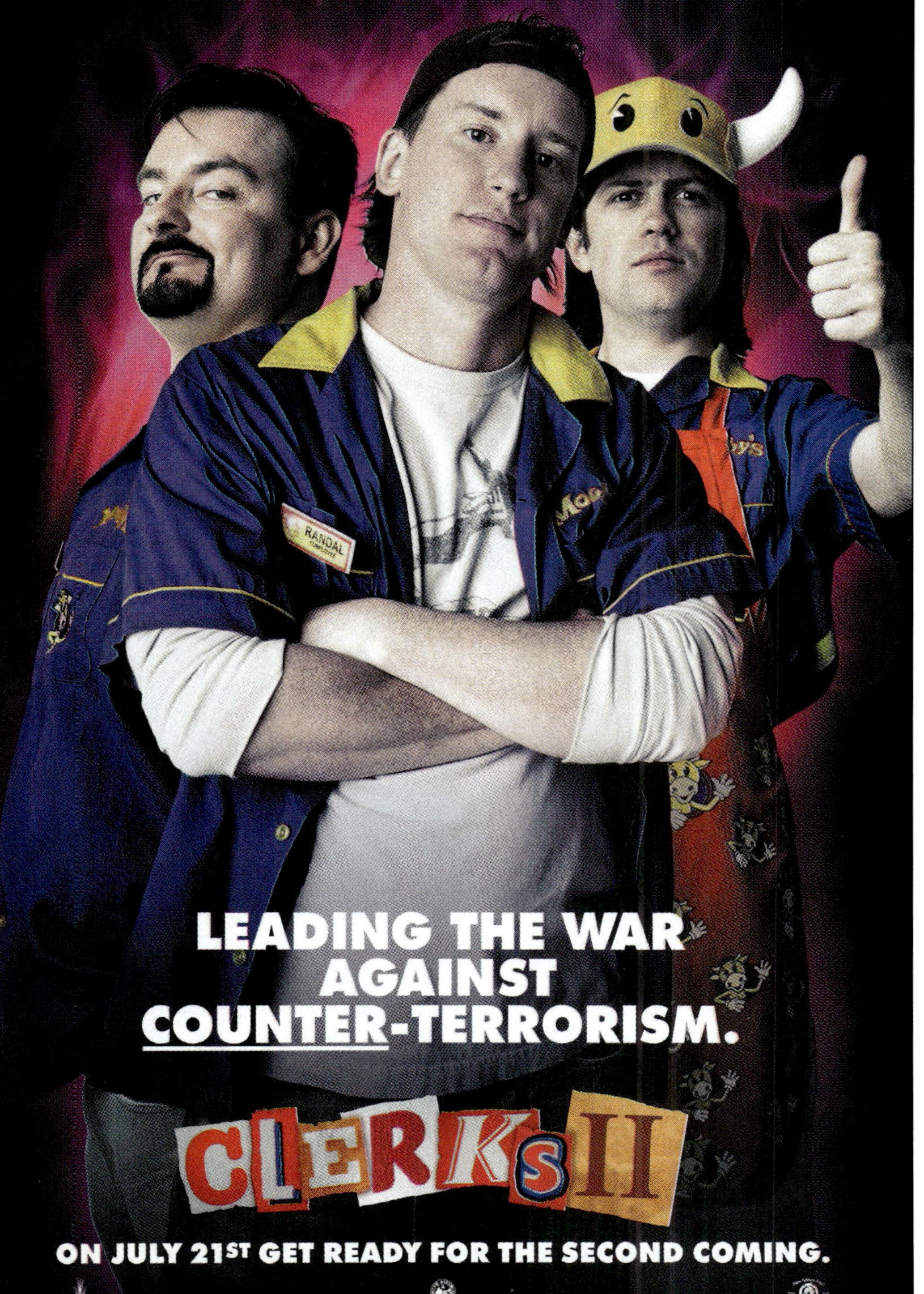

LEADING THE WAR
AGAINST
COUNTER-TERRORISM.
CLERKS II
ON JULY 21ST GET READY FOR THE SECOND COMING.
www.clerks2.com

STANDING FOR TRUTH.
STANDING FOR JUSTICE.
STANDING AROUND.
CLERKS II
ON JULY 21ST GET READY FOR THE SECOND COMING.
www.clerks2.com

RANDAL
Yeah. But don't worry. He made it. His pickle was small enough to stay wedged after only four bites.

LANCE
I'll bet you're the only guy in the world who still remembers that, Graves.

RANDAL
Oh, I'll bet you still remember it pretty vividly - Pickle-Fucker.

ELIAS
(to Lance)
Do you have any interest in building the ultimate fansite for both "The Lord of the Rings" and "The Transformers"? Because I'd moderate it for free.

RANDAL
Ease up, Pillow-Pants. The dude's not into your D&D/Go-Bots bullshit.

LANCE
Hey, hey, hey - don't insult the guy. The Go-Bots were like the K Mart Transformers.

ELIAS
Thank you. I keep telling him that.

LANCE
(hands Elias his card)
Here's my email address. Drop me a line with some of your ideas.

ELIAS
Cool!

Elias sneers at Randal and heads off. Lance looks up at the menu board, as Jay enters and does the same, looking for lunch.

LANCE
Now, let's see... What do I want? How 'bout a Skinny Calf with cheese and a Diet Coke.

RANDAL
I'll get your order.

29 INT BATHROOM - DAY

Tight on a urinal filled with piss-ice. A Mooby's cup is thrust into the piss-ice, scooping up a cup-full.

30 INT KITCHEN - DAY

The piss-ice filled cup is filled with soda.

31 INT BATHROOM - DAY

Tight on a fly strip as fingers pull dead flies from it.

32 INT KITCHEN - DAY

The flies are pressed into a sizzling burger patty by a spatula. Cheese is laid over the burning bugs.

33 INT MOOBY'S - DAY

Randal hands Lance his bag and cup of soda.

RANDAL
Here ya' go.

LANCE
That was fast.

RANDAL
And fresh. Thanks. Come again.

JAY
Yo! Let's wrap this up so I can get my Cow-Tipper on!

LANCE
(handing Jay his order, eyes locked on Randal)
Y'know what? Take mine. Something tells me I'm not gonna like it, am I?

Randal looks caught. Jay takes the food and drink excitedly, heading out.

JAY
Thanks, Pickle-Fucker!
(calling off to the OC Silent Bob)
YO! SOME PICKLE-FUCKER GAVE US FREE EATS!

Lance smiles at Dante and Randal.

LANCE
Y'know, I never eat fast food. It's not good for you. But when I heard you guys were actually working here... well, I just had to come in and see it for myself. It's kind of nice having that kind of free time. Just like it's kinda comforting to see how some things never change.
(shrugs as he heads off)
Take care, clerks.

Stung, Dante and Randal watch Lance go. He fires a pair of imaginary guns at them, then blows off the imaginary smoke.

LANCE
Oooo, sick burn.

He exits, laughing. Dante and Randal stand there, quietly. After a long beat, Randal hops over the counter.

RANDAL
Fuck this. Lemme borrow your car.

DANTE
You're supposed to be working...

RANDAL
I gotta get out of here for a few minutes! Lemme borrow your car!

Randal exits. Dante sighs and hops over the counter, following.

DANTE
Elias - tell Becky we'll be right back.

34 EXT MOOBY'S - DAY

With Dante trailing, Randal storms past Jay and Silent Bob.

DANTE
Where're we going?

Bob's sucking down the drink and Jay's digging into the burger. After a beat, both slowly stop drinking/chewing.

JAY
Yo, this tastes like piss and flies, don't it?

35 EXT TRACK - DAY

Tight on Dante and Randal.

DANTE
You sure you wanna do this?

RANDAL
Oh yeah. This'll make me feel better.

We cut out to reveal Dante and Randal positioned in go-karts at a shitty little round-about track. They both floor it and start tearing ass around the course.

Randal's in Heaven. His face is pure joy, as he cuts off little kids and Dante, leaving them in his dust. Dante, too, is having a pretty good time - smiling, and shaking his head at his friend's antics. For the moment, all is right in the world.

36 EXT HIGHWAY - DAY

Dante's car motors down the highway.

37 INT DANTE'S CAR - DAY

Dante is in a state of disbelief.

DANTE
Here's what I don't understand
about you: you have a license. You
can drive a grown-up car. And yet,
when you ride the go-karts, you
somehow feel better about yourself?

RANDAL
Look, it just centers me, alright?
Kinda the way jerking off in the
bathroom at work centers _you_.

DANTE
I only did it that one time. And
it wasn't to _center_ me.

RANDAL
Yeah, it was to cum. I don't know
about you, but cumming centers me.

DANTE
Then why'd we have to leave work
just so you could ride the go-karts
to clear your head?

RANDAL
Well I don't wanna jerk off in the
Mooby's _bathroom_. What if some
customer comes in and my jerking

off gets him all sex-nuts and retard strong, and suddenly, I'm fighting him off as he tries to jam my dick in his mouth?

DANTE

The likeliest of scenarios. Jesus - that shit Lance said must've really bothered you.

RANDAL

Oh, fuck him. He's an asshole. Always was. Now I'm sorry I let him bug me even for a second. At least I got a go-karts trip out of it.

DANTE

(beat)

Why do the go-karts help?

RANDAL

I don't know. The go-karts just remind me of a better time in my life.

DANTE

Like when?

RANDAL

Like when we were young and the world was still in front of us.

DANTE

We're not that old.

RANDAL

Yeah, but sometimes I feel like the world kind of left us behind a long time ago.

DANTE

(beat)

Y'know, you can do something about that.

RANDAL
I told you - I don't wanna jerk off
in the bathroom at work.

DANTE
No. I mean, you could get out of
Mooby's too. Completely change
your situation in life.

RANDAL
What'd be the point?
(looking out the window)
Besides - what do you give a shit?
You're leaving.

Dante tries to think of something to say, but can't. They drive in silence.

38 INT MOOBY'S - DAY

Dante and Randal enter to see Becky behind the counter, taking an order from a mid-'50's black HUSBAND and WIFE. Two other people are in line behind them. This is the Mooby's "rush".

BECKY
Thanks, y'know. Thanks. C'mon!

DANTE
I'm sorry.

Quickly, Dante hops the counter and starts prepping the order, as Randal heads into the kitchen.

DANTE
What do you need?

BECKY
(to Wife)
Was that a number two you wanted?

WIFE
Yeah. Bovine-sized.

BECKY
That'll be six eighty.
(calling back to Randal)
I need two Surlies and a Cow Tipper.

RANDAL
I'm on it.
(to Elias)
How're we set for fries?

Elias lifts the fry basket out of the fryer, revealing blackened, overcooked fries.

ELIAS
I don't think these look right, Randal.

RANDAL
Jesus! Step away from the fryer before you burn us all alive.

ELIAS
It's not my fault you abandoned your post.

RANDAL
Was it so much to ask that you handle the fries? The machine does all the work. What's, the machine gotta transform into some giant fucking robot before you'll take it seriously? Go home!

BECKY
Would you just make some new fries already.

WIFE
I don't have all night.

BECKY
Sorry, ma'am.

HUSBAND
(to Wife)
They need to get some Mexicans working in here. They'd be like...
(indicating speed)
ZIIIING!

WIFE
They don't play around.

HUSBAND
A Mexican made me lose my job. That motherfucker could put a roof up in thirty seconds.

BECKY
(to Dante)
Where the fuck did you guys go?

DANTE
You don't wanna know.

BECKY
I mean, I know it's your last day and all, but while you're still on the clock, can't you kinda pretend like you give a shit?

RANDAL
Don't blame this guy. Some cock stain we went to high school with showed up to remind us we're fucking failures, so I wanted to get out of here and blow off some steam, if you must know.

WIFE
(to Husband)
Did he say cock-stain? What's a cock-stain?

HUSBAND
That's some freaky white shit.

White boys get white women to do anything.
(quietly)
You wanna do a cock-stain?

BECKY
That's it? You know how many times I've seen people I went to school with come in here? Christ, one time I had to take the order of a guy I blew after the junior prom.

RANDAL
Yeah, I've waited on your brother too.

BECKY
I can't believe you - the smartest of smart asses - got rattled by some loser giving you shit about your McJob.

RANDAL
Oh, fuck him. Sooner or later, I'll do something with my life and make my mark. But until I do, whatever I do with my life is not a waste of time. It's all building toward something.

WIFE
How 'bout you build toward making those fries.

RANDAL
They're coming!

HUSBAND
(to Wife)
Remember, you're Saved. You can't be using that kind of language.

WIFE
(looking around)
Ain't nobody from my church in here.

RANDAL
(to Becky)
I don't mind people snickering at the stupid uniform I've gotta wear, but I'll be damned if I'm gonna let some self-righteous, lucky turd come in here and treat me and Dante like we're a couple of fucking porch-monkeys.

The Husband and Wife stop chatting amongst themselves and stare, wide-eyed, at Randal. Becky and Dante go wide-eyed. Randal looks around perplexed.

DANTE
RANDAL!
(to Wife)
I'm sorry! He's new!

WIFE
He really didn't say what I <u>think</u> he just said?

RANDAL
What - porch-monkeys?

BECKY
(to Randal, pissed)
What the fuck is wrong with you?!

WIFE
I want my money back right now!

BECKY
Of course. Please, take the food too - on us.

WIFE
Oh, no. I'm not eating something that was cooked by some cracker hate-monger!

HUSBAND
<u>I</u> will. Baby, you can't taste racism!

RANDAL
What racism? "Porch-monkey"?

WIFE
(lunges at Randal)
You little...

Randal recoils, ready for a fight. The Husband pulls the Wife back.

HUSBAND
C'mon baby, it ain't worth it!

WIFE
You're lucky my husband doesn't jump over this counter and knock your teeth out!

RANDAL
Why?

HUSBAND
Yeah, why? It's not like he called us porch-monkeys...

WIFE
(slaps his back)
Hey! HEY!

HUSBAND
Woman, stop hitting me! You remember what the judge said about putting your hands on people.

BECKY
(handing Wife her money)
Here, take this. This is your money. And take the food, please. We're so sorry.

WIFE
(pushing Husband to door)
I'm gonna write to the paper about this. You're all getting fired.

HUSBAND
(defiantly to Wife, as he
takes a bag of food)
I'm taking the food.

The Wife rushes her Husband, slaps the bag of food out his hands, and storms out. The Husband drags after her.

HUSBAND
DAMN!
(muttering under his breath)
Fucking porch-monkeys...

As they exit, Becky calls after them.

BECKY
Thanks. Come again!

Becky rears on Randal.

BECKY
Are you out of your fucking mind?!

RANDAL
What?! What's the big deal? Since when is it a crime to say porch monkey?

BECKY
Oh, I don't know. Since... forever!

RANDAL
Why?

DANTE
Because porch-monkey is a racial slur against black people!

RANDAL
No it's not. Nigger is.

BECKY
Jesus!

DANTE
RANDAL!

ELIAS
Did Randal just call Mr. Dante a nigger?

BECKY
Shut up, Elias!

RANDAL
I didn't call Dante a nigger - I just said that nigger is a racial slur.

DANTE
So is porch-monkey!

RANDAL
Oh, it is not. Coon, spook, spade, moolie, jigaboo, nig-nog - those are racial slurs. Porch-monkey is not.

BECKY
(exasperated)
I'm gonna try to forget this conversation ever happened. Elias, I want you to clean up that mess...
(up in Randal's grill)
And you are this close to getting shit-canned!
(storming off)
Fucking shoot me now!

Becky heads into her office and slams the door. Dante turns on Randal.

DANTE
What're you doing?! Are you trying to get fired?

RANDAL
When did porch-monkey suddenly become a racial slur?

DANTE
When ignorant racists starting saying it a hundred years ago.

RANDAL
Oh, bullshit. My grandmother used to call me a porch monkey all the time when I was a kid, because I'd sit on the porch and stare at my neighbors.

DANTE
Despite the fact that your grandmother used it as a term of endearment for you, it's still a racial slur. It'd be like your grandmother calling you "a little Kike".

RANDAL
Oh, it is not! Plus, my grandmother had nothing but the utmost respect for the Jewish community. When I was a kid, she told me to always treat the Jewish kids well, or else they'd put the Sheeny-curse on me.

DANTE
WHAT THE FUCK, MAN?!

RANDAL
What?

DANTE
SHEENY'S A RACIAL SLUR, TOO!

RANDAL
Oh, it is not.

DANTE
YES, IT IS!

RANDAL
Well she never called any Jews "Sheenies". She just used to say "Sheeny-curse" a lot. It was cute.

DANTE
It wasn't cute, it was racist!

RANDAL
I disagree, man. She was just an old timer. Everyone talked like that back then. It didn't mean they were racists.
(thinking back)
But my grandmother did once refer to a broken beer bottle as a "Nigger-Knife"...

Dante stares at Randal, open-mouthed and aghast.

RANDAL
Y'know, come to think of it, maybe my grandmother was kinda racist.

DANTE
YA' THINK?!

RANDAL
I still don't think porch-monkey should be considered a racist term. I've always used it to describe lazy people, not lazy black people. I think if we really tried, we can reclaim "porch-monkey" and save it.

DANTE
It can't be "saved", Randal! The sole purpose for its creation - the only reason it exists in the first place - is to disparage an entire race! And even if it could be saved, you can't save it because you're not black!

RANDAL
Well listen to you: telling me I can't do something because of the color of my skin. You're the racist.

Dante storms away, leaving Randal alone at the counter. Randal calls after him.

RANDAL
I'm taking it back. You watch.

Just then, a Mother and her little Kid approach the counter. Randal rubs the Kid's head, smiling.

RANDAL
What can I get for you today, ya' little porch-monkey?

Off the Mother's agog look.

RANDAL
It's cool, I'm taking it back.

39 INT BACK OFFICE - DAY

Becky sits at her desk, staring at the wedding invitation, thinking. She looks at her desk and sees a framed picture of her, Dante, Elias, and Randal. Dante has his arms around Becky. She eyes this for a beat, then heads out.

40 INT MOOBY'S - DAY

Dante sits at a table, reading the paper. Becky joins him.

BECKY
Hey.

DANTE
Hey.

BECKY
So are you scared about getting married at all?

DANTE
(looks around)
Were we in the middle of a conversation I don't remember leaving?

BECKY
I was just thinking about it, and I was thinking maybe you've been waiting for some friend to stop you from going through with the wedding by asking if you're even ready to go get married? So I'm asking: are you scared about getting married?

DANTE
(thinks)
Kinda. I'm not scared of getting married, y'know? I've always wanted to get married one day. But I'm scared of the wedding.

BECKY
Why?

DANTE
(beat)
I don't know how to dance.

BECKY
You're kidding.

DANTE
I wish I was.

BECKY
You're about to tie your life to someone - someone who doesn't really even get you as well as your friends do - and what you're sweating is dancing at the reception?

DANTE
I figure she'll eventually get me. You're married to a person long enough, they've gotta get you eventually, right?

BECKY
Are you kidding? My parents've been married for thirty five years, and they still don't get each other.

DANTE
Emma's pretty, smart, happy, a good person - and for some strange reason, she loves me.
What am I supposed to do - pass up on that because I've got a few stupid doubts and some jitters?

Becky's at a loss. Dante switches gears back.

DANTE
Besides, dancing at the reception's the more imperative concern at this point, because I only - presumably - get one chance to dance at my wedding.

BECKY
(giving up)
So, what - you can't slow dance?

DANTE
No. Anybody can slow dance. But this is one of the only times I'm ever gonna meet most of Becky's extended family. So I'd like to be able to show some flair on the dance floor, y'know? Like make an impression so maybe they'll kinda get whatever it is Emma sees in me, instead of all feeling like I'm

just some burger-peddling loser who
couldn't even bust a move.

Becky laughs.

DANTE

What?

BECKY

You're serious?

Dante nods. Becky studies Dante's face for a beat. She shakes her head and gets up, dragging Dante with her.

BECKY

Come on.

41 EXT MOOBY'S - DAY

Becky's face pops over the roof ledge, looking down at us.

BECKY

Hey! Twelve-step!

Jay, who leans against the building with Silent Bob, looks up, a bit caught off-guard.

OC BECKY

Jay!

JAY

(a bit nervous)

Lord?

OC BECKY

Up here, Jackass!

Jay moves away from the building and looks up at the roof, spotting Beck peering down at him.

JAY

'the fuck are you doing up there? Yo, if
you're gonna jump, lemme get a crack
at that pussy first! Lemme find out!

BECKY
You still got your boom-box?

Silent Bob appears next to the looking-up Jay. He extends the boom-box skyward for Becky to see.

BECKY
Play something and turn it way up!
Something dance-able!

Jay looks to Silent Bob, who shrugs. He holds the boom-box out to Jay to pick a tune.

42 EXT MOOBY'S ROOFTOP - SAME

Becky preps Dante to dance.

DANTE
Up here? You're gonna teach me to
dance up here?

BECKY
You want I should do it in front of
all the customers?

DANTE
What customers?

BECKY
(holds his hands)
Shut up. Get ready for the music.
You feel it here.
(taps his heart)
Here it comes...

Suddenly, King Diamond's "Welcome Home" blasts into their air, mid-song (at the "Grandma, what was it like?" lyrics). Becky and Dante startle.

43 EXT MOOBY'S - SAME

Jay and Silent Bob rock out.

44 EXT MOOBY'S ROOFTOP - SAME

Without moving, Becky calls out...

BECKY
SOMETHING A LITTLE LESS DEMONIC, PLEASE!

Suddenly, the music stops.

BECKY
THANK YOU!

Dante and Becky offer one another relieved eye-rolls. Then, The Jackson Five's "ABC" fills the air.

BECKY
Oh! This is perfect.
(to Dante)
Now just follow me.

DANTE
I'm trying.

Becky nods, starting to dance, forcing Dante to follow her moves. It's clear Dante really can't dance.

BECKY
Alright, you do suck. Sit down.

DANTE
I told you.

BECKY
Just watch.

Becky releases Dante, who steps back and watches Becky dance. We move in on Dante, captivated by Becky as she moves to the beat. This is who he should be with.

45 EXT MOOBY'S - SAME

Alone in the frame, Silent Bob starts dancing along with the music. Suddenly, Jay does the "Worm" through the frame.

46 INT MOOBY'S - SAME

At their seats, the CUSTOMERS start slightly boogying.

At the drive-thru window, Elias - headset in place - does a little DJ dancing bit, air-spining records.

Even Randal starts to bust a subtle move.

47 EXT MOOBY'S ROOFTOP - SAME

Becky pulls Dante back into her arms and gets him dancing.

48 EXT MOOBY'S - SAME

At the 1:44 break in the song ("Sit down, girl! I think I love ya'!") we start tight on a lip-syncing Silent Bob, then gradually pull back and crane up to reveal...

A parking lot full of backup dancers (roughly twenty) behind Jay and Silent Bob, all following the pair in a choreographed series of dance moves. It's a surreal, joyous release, communicating the idea that, if he wasn't before, Dante's really in love with Becky now.

49 INT MOOBY'S - SAME

Elias dances almost spastically now. Randal does the Randal/Wrangler across the front counter.

50 EXT MOOBY'S ROOFTOP - SAME

In a high wide, we see the ebullient Dante and Becky dancing, the dance troupe in the parking lot below.

As the song ends, Dante spins Becky into his arms, gazes down into her eyes, and says...

DANTE

I love you, Becky.

BECKY

I'm pregnant, Dante.

Dante drops Becky to the rooftop with a thud.

51 INT MOOBY'S - DAY

Randal sits at a table playing solitaire. Across the back of his Mooby's smock are scrawled the words "Porch-Monkey 4 Life". Dante sits in the seat across from Randal.

DANTE
I'm starting to have second thoughts.

RANDAL
About your sexuality?

DANTE
About going to Florida.

Randal looks at Dante. There's a beat of hopefulness. Then, Randal slips back into Randal-ness, as he shuffles the cards.

RANDAL
Yeah, right. Why now, all the sudden?

Dante tries to decide if he should share his news with Randal. He sighs. Then...

DANTE
Becky's pregnant.

RANDAL
(confused)
She is?
(shuffling in his hands)
So? What're ya' afraid you're gonna miss the baby shower?

DANTE
I'm the Father.

Randal loses control of the cards in his hands, spraying them out into the aisle, hitting a passing PATRON in the face, throwing the person, and their tray of trash, backwards over another table.

52 EXT MOOBY'S DUMPSTER - DAY

Jay takes a leak by the dumpster, with Bob keeping watch.

JAY
This sucks, man. I got public piss syndrome like a motherfucker. Be really fucking quiet.
(off Bob's glare)
Ew, dude - don't be looking at my dick!

Suddenly, the backdoor swings open, slamming into Jay.

JAY
SIR! MY BALLS!

Randal drags Dante outside and slams the door behind him.

RANDAL
What?!?

DANTE
We should probably help that guy...

RANDAL
Fuck him, man! How the fuck did you Father a child with a chick that's not your fiancé?
(suddenly wide-eyed)
Holy shit... She got pregnant off the toilet seat you jerked off onto, didn't she?! I fucking knew it!

DANTE
No. We had sex one night after work a few weeks ago.

RANDAL
Where?

DANTE
Here. On the prep table.

RANDAL
Ewww - that's my prep table.

DANTE
I don't know what I'm gonna do...

RANDAL
What'd Becks say?

DANTE
She wants to have it.

RANDAL
And she wants you to break it off with Emma and marry her?

DANTE
No.

RANDAL
She's gonna tell Emma?

DANTE
No.

RANDAL
Wait a sec - then what's the problem?

DANTE
Are you that dense?

RANDAL
No, seriously. If Becks isn't bustin' yer balls about it, then what's the big deal? You can still go down to Florida and live happily ever after.

DANTE
Knowing I've got a love-child up in Jersey?!

RANDAL
How the fuck do you always wind up with, like, two good looking chicks who want you? You're the most hideous fucking C.H.U.D. I've ever met, and you somehow always have a pair of girls fighting over you.

DANTE
(suddenly turning on him)
Listen, you can never tell anybody about this!

RANDAL
Who'm I gonna tell?

DANTE
I'm serious, Randal! And not just for me - Becky said she doesn't want anyone to know.

RANDAL
Then what'd you tell me for?

DANTE
You've fucked me over in the past, but this is huge. This is serious. Promise me you'll keep your mouth shut! Because if you fuck me over this time, I swear to God, I'll beat the shit out of you!

RANDAL
You and what army?

DANTE
(grabbing him)
I'm serious!

RANDAL
I'm serious, too - you and what army?

DANTE
(shaking him)
Promise me!

RANDAL
(pushing Dante away)
Alright! Get offa me, you nut!

Suddenly, just as Jay's getting back up, the back door swings open again, slamming him into the wall anew.

JAY
WHAT THE FUCK?!?

Becky's standing there. She's looking at Dante and Randal. They both look caught. After a beat...

BECKY
Can I talk to you?

DANTE
Sure. We were just...

RANDAL
(blurting it out)
May your first child be a masculine child!

Becky looks at Randal, shocked, then to Dante, hurt. She rushes back inside. Dante turns on Randal.

DANTE
RANDAL!?!

RANDAL
She was sweating me, man! It just came out!

Not listening to him, Dante swings at Randal. Randal ducks, and Dante winds up punching the drive-thru menu board.

DANTE
AHHH - FUCK!

RANDAL
You swung at me!

DANTE
(holding his hand)
You ducked?!

RANDAL
Because you swung at me!

DANTE
Dammit!

Dante rushes inside, quickly followed by Randal. Slowly, Jay and Silent Bob pop their heads up from behind the dumpster.

53 INT MOOBY'S - DAY

Dante rushes in through the kitchen, holding his fist. He passes Elias, who's desperately trying to wrap a bunch of poorly-made burgers, as three Customers wait.

DANTE
Where's Becky?

ELIAS
She just left. I need help here, Mr. Dante! I can't wrap good, and Randal ate the last pickles!

RANDAL
(passing Elias)
You fucking snitch.

ELIAS
I'm sorry, Randal, I'm sorry!

54 EXT MOOBY'S - DUSK

Dante rushes out of the restaurant just as Becky's car screeches out of the parking lot.

DANTE
BECKY!!!

But she's gone. Randal joins Dante. After a beat...

RANDAL
Maybe she went to get a home pregnancy test. Just to be sure.

DANTE
(absently)
How the fuck could this day get any worse?

On cue, a pickup truck towing a single-hole horse trailer pulls into the parking lot. Randal goes wide-eyed.

RANDAL
Well what the fuck are you doing, man?! Go after her!

DANTE
Ya' think?

RANDAL
(pushing him toward car)
Damn right I do. You two've gotta work this out. Follow her and talk to her for an hour, then come back here.

DANTE
An hour?

RANDAL
(opening his car door)
I've always found that any more time than that and you run the risk of saying the wrong thing again. Follow her, talk to her for an hour, then come back here and help me close up.

DANTE
This is kinda important. You can't close up by yourself?!

RANDAL
Fuckin', man... you're gonna be a Father soon. Time to start acting responsibly. Be back in an hour.

Randal slams the door closed. Bewildered, Dante starts the car and backs out. Randal waves at him as he pulls out of the parking lot, then saunters over to trailer-towing pickup truck just in time to meet the DRIVER.

RANDAL
Hello. I take it you're with Kinky Kelly?

DRIVER
Good guess. You Randal?

RANDAL
I am. How long you need to set up?

DRIVER
I just gotta hook up the boom-box and hang a few curtains and some lights. I got a small smoke machine, for ambience.

RANDAL
You might as well start setting up. We've got about an hour before the guest of honor gets back.
(looking around)
So do I get to meet Kelly before the show or what?

DRIVER
Nah. Kelly kinda likes privacy before showtime. But after the show, if you want, for an extra five hundred, you can fuck Kelly.

RANDAL
Really? Sweet!

DRIVER
Yeah. So where we doing this thing?

RANDAL
Right in the restaurant.

DRIVER
You're kidding.

RANDAL
Not spacious enough?

DRIVER
No, it's plenty spacious. Just... kinda weird, ain't it?

RANDAL
"Kinda weird"? You're in the bestiality business, dude.

DRIVER
Hey, Fucko. We like to call it Inter-Species Erotica.

RANDAL
Intriguing.

55 MONTAGE - NIGHT

To The Smashing Pumpkins' "1979", we check in on all of our main characters, at this last moment before all their lives change forever.

Dante drives around town, looking for any sign of Becky, but more lost in thought about his future.

Becky pulls up in front of a Women's Clinic, weighing her options.

As the Driver sets up a stage, Randal sits on a table top, staring out the restaurant windows. Alone with his thoughts, this is the most contemplative we've ever seen Randal Graves.

Emma frosts a cake, all in love.

Elias mops up.

Dante again. He rolls to a stop at a red light and glances out his driver's side window, spotting...

A RESTAURANT - like a diner. Through a window, we see a family sitting around a table, eating: Mom, Dad, and Toddler. The Toddler is leaning tummy-side against the booth, looking out the window at...

Dante - who stares back. We cut back and forth between the two, getting in closer and closer on their faces. Finally, the Kid presses her face into window and smiles at Dante. Dante smiles back, warmly - not so much at the kid, as the idea of a kid. Dante waves. The Kid waves back.

And with that, his decision is made.

56 EXT MOOBY'S - LATER

Dante's car pulls into the parking lot. He gets out and starts heading toward Mooby's when we hear the music: pulse pounding techno. He looks to the restaurant and sees...

The windows fogged up by smoke coming from inside.

DANTE

Oh, no. Not again...

Dante pulls his cell phone and dials 911 as he races toward the building.

DANTE

Yeah, I've got a fire at Mooby's on
Memorial Parkway in Leonardo.

57 INT MOOBY'S - SAME

Dante rushes in to see a decidedly different Mooby's than he left: pink silks are hung from the ceiling to give a harem environment-like effect. There's a flashing light display and a disco ball hanging from the ceiling. The hallway by the bathrooms/kitchen door is curtained off. A small smoke machine creates "atmosphere." Jay and Silent Bob wave at Dante from across the room, party favors in their mouths.

The excited-as-a-school-kid Randal joins Dante. He holds two beers.

DANTE
(yelling over the music)
What the fuck's going on?!

RANDAL
It's your going away party!

A piss-drunk Elias pops up from behind Jay and Silent Bob.

ELIAS
We'sh all gonna get drunk and get laid! WOOOOOOO!!!

DANTE
(shocked)
Oh my God - is Elias hammered?!

JAY
Isn't it awesome? My man smoked three blunts fulla skunk!

ELIAS
Fuck Pillow-Pants! Honk if you love or like pussy!

The inebriated Elias falls off the table.

JAY
(to Silent Bob)
Yo, we love pussy!

Jay and Silent Bob blow into their party horns.

Dante looks at the unlikely trio, flabbergasted. Randal shoves a beer into Dante's hand.

RANDAL
Tonight, before you leave me forever, we're gonna peep something together we've been talking about since we saw "Bachelor Party" on Beta at your parents' house when we were twelve!

DANTE
What are you talking about?

RANDAL
(raises his beer to Dante)
I'm gonna miss you, man.

DANTE
I'm gonna miss you too, but this is a little much.

RANDAL
Yeah? Just wait.

Randal heads over to the curtained off area and pokes his head in, shares a few words, then pulls it out again.

RANDAL
Showtime! Ladies and gentlemen! And you, Elias! Straight from the debauchery captiol of the world - Tijuana, Mexico...!

Dante suddenly starts piecing it together.

DANTE
Oh God, no...

RANDAL
Oh God, yes!

Randal snaps his fingers and an insane lighting display bathes the restaurant in a blue/purple haze.

RANDAL
Get ready for some hardcore bestiality...

DRIVER
(from behind curtain)
Inter-species erotica, Fucko!

RANDAL
...Inter-species erotica at its finest!
Straight from T.J., I give you
KINKY KELLY AND THE SEXY STUD!!!

Randal quickly heads off, and the Driver and a DONKEY trot out from behind the curtain. The Driver is dressed in hardcore gay leather gear, and gyrates to the music. The donkey looks around vacantly.

Dante looks to the smiling Randal.

RANDAL
Don't worry, the chick's coming.

As the Driver dances seductively at the donkey, Randal, Dante, Jay, Silent Bob, and Elias watch with varied expressions. Slowly, realization starts to set in, and Randal's smile starts to drop a bit, as he puts it together.

RANDAL
Any minute now, the chick's coming...

The Driver starts air-grinding at the donkey's face, thrusting suggestively.

Elias still wears a drunken grin. Jay looks at Silent Bob, then at Randal. Dante looks to Randal too.

JAY
That guy's being awfully forward with that donkey.

DANTE
Uh, Randal...

RANDAL
Where the fuck's the chick?!

Randal rushes the Driver, trying to talk to him while the Driver continues to boogie sexually at the mule.

RANDAL
Yo! Freddie fucking Mercury!
Where's Kinky Kelly?

DRIVER
(nuzzling the mule)
Right here.

RANDAL
(off the donkey)
I thought that's the "sexy stud"?

DRIVER
I'm the sexy stud.

RANDAL
(checking first)
But this donkey's a dude!

DRIVER
Kelly can be a guy's name too.
Hey!

Randal stares at the Driver as he boogies off, then shrugs in agreement, rejoining the group.

RANDAL
Uh... due to some nomenclature confusion, there's not gonna be any chick.

JAY
Then who the fuck's gonna blow the donkey?

All look OC.

The Driver drops to his knees under the donkey, mouth heading for the donkey dick.

All assembled look on horrified yet transfixed. All except Elias, who's still smiling.

ELIAS
I've got a huge boner right now!

Suddenly, BECKY enters the restaurant. She looks around then sees the donkey show. She goes wide-eyed.

BECKY
Oh... my... God...

Dante spots Becky and races over to her.

DANTE
Where did you go?

BECKY
What the fuck's going on here?

DANTE
Uh... inter-special erotica. Are you okay?

BECKY
I'm disgusted and repulsed... but I can't look away.

Dante drags Becky outside, as she stares back at the Donkey Show over her shoulder.

BECKY
That's huge!

Randal, Jay, Silent Bob, and Elias watch the OC donkey show as well, and all tilt their heads in unison at the same angle to get a better, horrified view of the action.

58 EXT MOOBY'S - SAME

Dante and Becky emerge. Becky's still looking back at the weirdness as the doors close behind them.

DANTE
We've gotta talk.

BECKY
(dazed)
Did you see the size of that cock?

DANTE
I love you.

Becky's attention snaps to Dante. She's unable to speak.

DANTE
And I think you love me too.

BECKY
(beat)
Of course. I mean, we're friends.

DANTE
I think you love me as more than a friend.

Becky won't let herself speak. She just looks at Dante.

DANTE
You can say it.

BECKY
But I don't believe in romantic love.

DANTE
I think you do.

BECKY
Do you really wanna do this right now?

59 INT MOOBY'S - SAME

We're on Randal, Jay, Silent Bob and Elias, kinda staring just below frame. Then, the Driver pops up into the frame as if he's just gotten up, facing us. He wipes his mouth, still gyrating to the music.

RANDAL
Whelp. I guess the show's over.

JAY
I don't think so, sir...

Randal follows Jay's stunned gaze back to the OC Driver.

Below frame, the Driver seems to be pulling his cock out of his leathers. He spits forcefully into his hand, dipping his hand below frame to rub it into his unseen cock.

Jay and crew are starting to catch on.

ELIAS
(unbuttoning his pants)
If he's gonna jerk off, then I'm gonna jerk off too.

RANDAL
(horrified)
I don't think he's gonna jerk off.

The Driver dances around to the back of the donkey. Sexily, he grabs the donkey's hips.

60 EXT MOOBY'S - SAME

Jay bursts out of the restaurant, addressing Dante and Becky.

JAY
Yo, you guys're gonna miss this shit! The big guy's gonna cornhole that ass! With his weiner!

Jay rushes back inside.

BECKY
(to Dante)
Hold that thought.

Becky rushes back inside, quickly followed by Dante.

61 INT MOOBY'S - SAME

Dante and Becky enter, staring at the OC show, wide-eyed.

In beat with the music, the Driver, is doing pelvic thrusts behind the donkey.

A drunken Elias smiles.

ELIAS
I hope that donkey doesn't have a Hiney-Troll.

Dante and Becky stare, shocked, at the OC weirdness.

BECKY
Alright, I do.

DANTE
Do what?

BECKY
I do love you.

Dante looks to Becky. Becky looks at Dante. The pair kiss, urgently.

Jay, Silent Bob and Randal stare agog at the OC Dante and Becky.

JAY
What kinda crazy fuck gets that turned on watching a guy fuck a donkey?

Silent Bob nudges Jay and points to OC.

Elias spanks below the frame, staring hungrily at the OC donkey show, crying.

ELIAS

I'm sorry Jesus... UHHHN!

Becky and Dante continue to kiss. We pan over to reveal EMMA standing in the restaurant doorway holding the cake she made, mouth agape.

EMMA

Dante?

Dante and Becky break their kiss to see Emma. They're so fucking caught.

EMMA

What's... what's going on?

The Driver, also, looks at the OC Emma.

DRIVER

Ooo! Cake!

Emma looks disgustedly at the donkey show for a moment, then to Dante and Becky, hurt. Suddenly, Jay joins her, slapping her on the back.

JAY

Yo! I was taking a piss outside
when I heard the news. Congrats!

Emma looks at him, confused.

JAY

You're gonna have a baby, ain'tcha?

EMMA

No. Who said that?

Jay looks to Dante and Becky, then looks down, sort of embarrassed, realizing he's spoken when he shouldn't have.

JAY
(trying to play it off)
Um... some asshole.

Emma's attention suddenly snaps to Dante and Becky. Both look a little more caught. Emma goes wide-eyed, grabbing her stomach. She hands the cake off to Jay and slowly crosses to Dante, who holds her by the shoulders, ashamed.

DANTE
I'm sorry.

Exploding, Emma knees Dante in the balls. Dante drops to his knees, holding his groin in agony. Jay hands her the cake.

JAY
Quick! Hit that two-timing fuck with this!

For good measure, Emma smashes the cake into Dante's face, knocking him backwards. Jay eyes Emma.

JAY
You wanna go out some time?

Emma rolls her eyes, then her attention snaps to Becky.

BECKY
Emma... I don't know what to say.

EMMA
(pulling off the ring)
Take him, you fucking whore.

Emma throws her engagement ring at Becky and storms out. Dante tries to move to follow her, but as Emma exits, he sees through the windows...

A fire truck and a cop car pulling up.

Jay also sees this and reacts, racing over to Silent Bob and Randal.

JAY

Yo, the cops are here, we're holding, and I'm still on probation.

Silent Bob hops off the table and tries to drag Randal away with him and Jay, to avoid arrest.

Becky, too, heads off.

As Dante looks on wide-eyed, Firemen race into the restaurant, followed by two Cops, one of whom is black. They screech to a stop, horrified as they take in the scene.

FIREMAN

What the fuck...?!

BLACK COP

(off Randal's shirt)

"Porch-monkey"?

RANDAL

It's cool. I'm taking it back.

Elias runs through the frame, pants down, screaming...

ELIAS

WOOOO!!! I LOVE PUSSY AND BEER!

62 EXT POLICE STATION - NIGHT

An establishing shot.

63 INT JAIL CELLS - SAME

Dante and Randal are in one cell. Jay and Silent Bob are in another. The sleeping Elias and the Driver are in separate cells.

Jay and Silent Bob look around the cell, then at each other.

JAY

Deja fuckin' vu, right?

Silent Bob nods.

Randal studies the cell he's in with Dante. Dante looks shell-shocked.

RANDAL
(off bars)
The jail cell design hasn't changed much in centuries, has it? Maybe it's time they brought in the laser bars or something.

Randal looks to Dante for some kind or response. Dante says nothing; he just stares forward, blankly. From the next cell, Jay obliges.

JAY
They could make a hard plastic cage, like Magneto's in "X-Men 2." Nong.

RANDAL
C'mon, man - let's keep it in the real world, alright?
(thinks)
But you know what wouldn't be a bad idea? Carbonite.
(to Dante)
What do you think, Dante?

Dante leaps at Randal, slamming him against the prison bars, his hands around Randal's neck.

DANTE
I THINK I WANNA KILL YOU!

RANDAL
GET... OFFA ME!

DANTE
YOU'VE RUINED MY LIFE!

RANDAL
YOUR LIFE... WAS ALREADY... RUINED!

On "ruined", Randal uses all his might to push Dante off him, throwing him backwards into the prison bars. Jay hangs off his prison bars like a monkey, watching excitedly.

JAY
WHAT UP?! STEEL CAGE MATCH!

Dante and Randal square off opposite one another defensively for a beat.

DANTE
What the fuck were you thinking? A fucking Donkey Show?!

RANDAL
It was your going away present!

DANTE
It sure was! I just never thought I'd be going away to prison!

DRIVER
Uh, boys? You can't be imprisoned for watching an inter-species sex act. You guys'll walk, and the most I'll get is a fine for animal abuse and a lot of disgusted looks from conservative asswipes who can't appreciate sexual exploration. Hey!

DANTE
(to Randal)
I can't believe you. I finally get my shit together, I'm hours from getting out of here and really starting my life, and you somehow figured out a way to obliterate all that and reduce me to a convict!

RANDAL
Yeah, it's my fault your life's fucked up. I'm the engaged guy who knocked up my boss.

JAY
You knocked up that guy who owns Mooby's?

RANDAL
(laughing at the misunderstanding)
What?

DANTE
(to Jay)
Would you shut up?
(to Randal)
You're chaos incarnate, man. Our whole lives, you've been getting me into trouble and holding me back.

RANDAL
Oh, I'm holding you back. I remember like ten years ago, the night we went to Julie Dwyer's funeral, you were all like "I'm gonna shit or get off the pot."

DANTE
You said "shit or get off the pot", not me.

RANDAL
You got all fired up about taking charge of your life, and what'd you do? You worked at the store 'til the place burned down.

DANTE
I took courses at Brookdale.

RANDAL
And dropped out.

DANTE
Because you stopped going!

RANDAL
Because we were just killing time with those classes! One semester we took Criminology, fer Chrisakes! What the fuck were we training to be - Batman?

DANTE
At least we were doing something, instead of wasting our time in a fucking convenience store.

RANDAL
You can bad-mouth Quick Stop all you want, but I miss that place. I loved working there. I look back on that period as the best time of my life.

DANTE
Now I know you're fucking nuts.

RANDAL
Why? Because I enjoyed what I did? I got to watch movies, fuck with assholes, and hang out with my best friend all day long - can you think of a better way to make a living? Sure, it may not've been what "everyone does", but it was pretty fucking good!

DANTE
Man, that's you all over: scrape by with the bare minimum. Well I'm tired of that, Randal. I'm not in high school anymore. Shit, I'm not even in my twenties anymore. I don't wanna sit around and rag on customers while eating free food. That's what you want. That's what you've always wanted. Well if that's all you want out of life, then God bless. But I refuse to

let your shit taint the rest of mine. No - I'm gonna smooth things over with Emma, go to Florida, and start my Randal Graves-free existence!
(sitting)
And try to forget the last thirty three years ever happened.

Randal looks at Dante, stung. After a long beat...

RANDAL
So that's how you see all this time we've spent together?

Randal shakes his head, stifling a depressed chuckle.

RANDAL
It's weird. I always thought you were the only person in the world who got me and had my back. The only guy who'd take a bullet for me. 'Cause I assumed you felt the same way about me that I feel about you. And then one day, you're all the sudden like "I'm moving. Bye." You know what that's been like for me? I'm looking at a future that just... sucks - because you're not gonna be in it anymore. And you're not even throwing me over for a life that means something to you. It's just this stupid, hollow existence you think you should embrace 'cause you're getting old or something - because it's the kinda life everyone else goes after. You're a fucking drone.

DANTE
Fine. The next friend whose life you ruin can be a totally free spirit. How's that?

RANDAL
You think I wanna start making new friends at my age? Christ, who'd want me as their friend? I hate everyone and everything seems stupid to me. But you were always the counter-balance to that - the guy who was always like the ying to my yang. But now what the fuck am I gonna do for the rest of my life? I mean, shit - I really wish you would've told me when we first met that one day you were gonna bail on our friendship. Because if I knew you were just gonna flake on me a few decades later, I wouldn't've even bothered with your ass in the first place!

Randal turns away from Dante, maybe trying not to choke up. Dante's flabbergasted. Then, out of the silence, comes...

JAY
Jesus - why don't you two just fuck and get it over with.
(as an afterthought)
Faggots.

DANTE
Why can't you ever say something useful for a change?

Jay mean-mugs Dante, then looks to Silent Bob.

JAY
Well? The fuck are you waitin' for. That's your cue, Fat-ass.

Silent Bob thinks for a beat, then...

SILENT BOB
I got nothing.

JAY

Jesus Christ! What the fuck good are you, ya' mute-fuck.

SILENT BOB

You know what? That hurts. What the fuck good are <u>you</u>? You got like one answer for everything: "Pussy, man!"

RANDAL

(off Dante)

Oh, man - then you must love this guy, 'cause he's the biggest pussy I ever met: the dude who lives his life according to <u>other</u> people's standards. "I've gotta go to Florida and get married, 'cause that's what expected of me." And the insane part is he ain't even that crazy about the chick he's marrying <u>or</u> Florida. Never mind the fact that he's got a perfectly good chick right here in Jersey who he's nuts about, and even Anne fucking Frank could see she's nuts about him, God knows why! And she likes you for who you are, man. She ain't trying to stuff you into a box you'll never fit into! If you had any fucking sense whatsoever, you'd stop trying to bray it up with the rest of the fucking sheep, and do what makes sense for <u>you</u>, you fucking ass!

DANTE

Oh yeah? And what's that? You've obviously got such a great handle on <u>your</u> life, tell me what you'd do if you were in <u>my</u> position! Or even what you'd do in your position! Swing that judgmental pendulum back the other way and tell me how you'd solve all your problems, asshole! What the fuck would the great Randal Graves do if he were half the master of his own destiny that I'm supposed to be?!

RANDAL

I'D BUY THE QUICK STOP AND RE-OPEN IT MYSELF!

Dante's attention snaps to. Holy shit: the closet nihilist harbors a dream.

RANDAL

That's what I'd do! That's what we should do!

DANTE

Ch'yeah, right - who're we, Lance Dowds? You know how much it'd cost to buy Quick Stop and re-build it? Fifty grand, easily. And neither of us've got that kinda money.

Dante and Randal deflate, reality creeping back in. All is quiet. Then...

OC JAY

We do.

Dante and Randal look to Jay and Silent Bob. Jay nods at the pair.

JAY

That's right.

Dante and Randal stare at Jay and Bob, perplexed.

RANDAL

And you'd be willing to lend us some of that money to re-open the stores?

JAY
Sure. But on two conditions: one, we get to hang out in front of the stores all we want and you can never call the cops on us. And two... you've gotta blow each other and let us watch. Then you gotta go ass-to-mouth.

Silent Bob shakes his head "No" to Jay. Jay rethinks his offer.

JAY
Alright - just the first condition.

RANDAL
(to Dante)
What do you think?

DANTE
I almost hate to say it... but it kinda makes sense.

RANDAL
Maybe that's why we spent so much time in that store - and why college or anything else never panned out for us. I mean, think about it: you and me running our own business instead of working for some other asshole? It could be pretty fucking sweet, right?

DANTE
Yeah, it really could...
(shakes his head)
But I don't know, man. I was this close to starting a new life...

RANDAL
Jesus... You're really gonna make me do this, aren't you?
(to Jay and Bob)
Can you guys do me a favor and cover your ears?

Jay and Bob cover their ears.

A much different, much more serious Randal looks to Dante. He swallows hard. Then...

RANDAL
You're my best friend. And I love you.
(beat; then quickly)
In a totally hetero way.

JAY
(ears still covered)
Sh'yeah, right...

RANDAL
(to Dante; glassy-eyed)
Please, man - don't leave me.

We hold on Dante for a long beat. Then...

64 EXT BANK - DAY

Dante and Randal head inside.

65 INT BANK - DAY

A DEED is stamped.

The BANKER pushes the Deed across the desk to Dante and Randal, who look at it, smile. Randal extends his hand to Dante for a handshake, and Dante pulls Randal into a hug.

66 EXT QUICK STOP - DAY

Dante and Randal pull down the boards that cover the burnt out store, then head inside.

67 INT QUICK STOP - DAY

A sweaty Dante and Randal work on re-building the store.

68 EXT MOOBY'S DRIVE-THRU WINDOW - DAY

A car pulls up and Becky opens the window, plopping an order on the ledge without looking up.

69 INT MOOBY'S DRIVE THRU WINDOW - SAME

Reading off the receipt, Becky doesn't look at her customer.

BECKY
That'll be nine eighty.

Becky absently sticks her hand out the window for payment.

Tight on the opened ring box sporting a modest engagement ring that's placed in her palm.

Becky looks to her hand, momentarily perplexed, until she sees the box and its contents. She quickly looks up to see who's responsible.

Dante sits in the driver's seat, smiling at her.

DANTE
You already taught me how to dance at a wedding.

Becky starts to tear up.

DANTE
I mean, I know you don't believe in romantic love...

Becky dives through the drive-thru window, hanging into Dante's car, kissing him big time. They break for a beat.

DANTE
Is that a yes?

BECKY
What took you so long?

The pair go back to kissing.

Leaning on the drive-thru window, Elias watches them, smiling. Then...

ELIAS
"One ring to rule them all..."

70 INT RST VIDEO - DAY

Tight on an application being slid across the counter.

We go wide to reveal Elias standing opposite the counter of Dante and Randal in the the nearly complete video store. The pair study the application for a beat, then look at one another, then to Elias, then back at each other. Dante shakes his head "yes" but Randal shakes his head "no." Dante offers him a "C'mon..." kinda look. Randal look Elias up and down, then shrugs and nods. Elias leaps across the counter, hugging Randal. Randal's trying to back him off.

71 EXT QUICK STOP - DAY

The stores complete, Dante and Randal are on ladders, hanging another sign over the windows that reads "I Assure You, We're Open." A starting-to-show Becky is down below, directing them how to hang the sign straight, standing beside Elias. Dante and Randal climb down from their ladders, step back, and admire their handi-work. Becky gives Dante a hug. Randal pats Dante on the back.

72 EXT RST VIDEO - DAY

It's quiet. Then, Jay and Silent Bob enter. They find their position against the RST wall and try to settle in, unsuccessfully. Then, Silent Bob exits the frame and returns with a boom-box. He sets it down and presses play. "Goodbye Horses" fills the air.

JAY
Oh!

Jay starts to dance, pulling out his Chapstick and applying it like lipstick.

73 INT QUICK STOP - DAY

Dante and Randal take their places behind the counter in the standard two-shot. Satisfied with all the work they've done and accomplished, the pair settle into their positions, sighing with a smile.

RANDAL
You know what?

DANTE
What?

RANDAL
You're not even supposed to be here today.

Dante smiles. Randal cracks open a Slim-Jim.

DANTE
Can you feel it?

RANDAL
Feel what?

DANTE
Today's the first day of the rest of our lives.

The pair nod, then relax, looking around the store with a smile. Soul Asylum's "Misery" starts to play. As we slowly pull back, Dante and Randal's smiles start to drop as they realize what they've done, and the color in the shot drains to BLACK & WHITE. Somehow, amazingly, these guys are right back where they started.

THE END

Unit Production Manager
MARJORIE ERGAS

First Assistant Director
TONY STEINBERG

Second Assistant Director
HEATHER DENTON

CAST
(in order of appearance)

Dante	BRIAN O'HALLORAN
Randal	JEFF ANDERSON
Jay	JASON MEWES
Silent Bob	KEVIN SMITH
Teen #1	JAKE RICHARDSON
Teen #2	ETHAN SUPLEE
Counter Girl with Ear Guy	RACHEL LARRATT
Ear Guy	SHANNON LARRATT
Emma	JENNIFER SCHWALBACH
Gawking Guy	BEN AFFLECK
Catholic Schoolgirls	SARAH AULT
	LALIDA SUJJAVASIN
Elias	TREVOR FEHRMAN
Elias' Mom	GAIL STANLEY
Elias' Dad	BRUCE MACINTOSH
Concerned Father	SCOTT MOSIER
Becky	ROSARIO DAWSON
Hobbit Lover	KEVIN WEISMAN
Diner 1	STEVEN RAU
Diner 2	MIKE TSUCALAS
Lance Dowds	JASON LEE
Husband	EARTHQUAKE
Wife	WANDA SYKES
Customer 1	JOEY FIGUEROA
Customer 2	MIKE CECCONI
Tumbling Customer	ETHAN JENSEN
Sexy Stud	ZAK KNUTSON
Kid in Window	HARLEY QUINN SMITH
Cop	KEVIN MICHAEL RICHARDSON
Fireman	ED JANDA
Bank Manager	BYRON STANLEY
Pack-o-Smokes Guy	WALTER FLANAGAN
Milk Maid	GRACE SMITH
Stunt Coordinator	GARY JENSEN

Stunts	ETHAN JENSEN
	JESSI JENSEN
	KOFI YIADOM
Stunt Kid #1	GINO WOULARD
Stunt Kid #2	KANAN HOOKER
Stunt Kid #3	HOUSTON HOOKER
Becky Stunt Double	TRACY KEEHN DASHNAW
Art Director	MARK FISICHELLA
Set Decorator	SUSAN LYNCH
Graphic Consultant	R. SCOTT PURCELL
Choreographer	MICHAEL ROONEY
Assistant Choreographer	MARTY KUDELKA
A-Camera Operator	ANDY GRAHAM
First Assistant A-Camera	PAUL MALETICH
Second Assistant A-Camera	AARON BOWEN
B-Camera Operators	RENATO DI GIUSEPPE
First Assistant B-Camera	SAL CONIGLIO
C-Camera Operator	SCOTT KAYE
First Assistant C-Camera	JAMES MATLOSZ
Camera Loader /Second Assistant B-Camera	Q EDWARDS
Steadicam Operator	RICK DAVIDSON
First Assistant Steadicam	JOSH HARRISON
Script Supervisor	CAROL BANKER
Production Sound Mixer	WHIT NORRIS, C.A.S.
Boom Operator	C. DOUGLAS CAMERON
Sound Utility Operator	KAT CRAIG
Audio Playback	GARY RAYMOND
Gaffer	JEREMY GRAHAM
Best Boy Electric	BOB SHOEMAKER
Electricians	NICK AIELLO
	CARL FLOOD
	BILL REILLY
	ALEX SZUCH
	JARROD HEATH
	DAVID MCGRORY
Key Grip	OTTO E. BETANCOURT
Best Boy Grip	CHAD DIEKMANN
Dolly Grips	JOHN MARTIN
	JAMES JOHNSON

Grips	MATT CRAPO
	JAY POPE
	CHRIS MOORE
Costume Supervisor	KIA TYRRELL
Key Set Costumer	AMY FEGELY
Set Costumer	CHRISTINE HAWES
Costume Production Assistant	MAYUMI MASAOKA
Key Makeup Artist	AMY HARMON
	TRICIA SAWYER
Assistant Makeup	BROOKE BELLE
Key Hairstylists	NICOLE VENABLES
	JANINE RATH-THOMPSON
Assistant Hairstylist	SARAH AULT
Property Master	LISA DE ALVA
Assistant Property Master	RICH ROBINSON
Additional Assistant Property Masters	BRUCE MINK
	SAL VALLE
Special Effects	CHARLIE BELARDINELLI
Production Coordinator	MARK ASARO
Assistant Production Coordinator	JENNIFER SCOTT
Production Secretary	DANNY MUSCOPLAT
Second Second Assistant Director	SEPTEMBER DEATH
Production Accountant	MARY JASIONOWSKI
Assistant Accountant	NICHOLAS MONAHAN
Post Production Accountant	JULIE HANSEN
	FILM AUDITORS, INC.
Assistant to Kevin Smith	GAIL STANLEY
Office Production Assistants	JACOB WEISMAN
	MARK PIERCE
	ARTURO ALAMO
	LAURA GUZIK
	ANTOINETTE ACHUCARRO
Key Set Production Assistant	AARON KINSER
Set Production Assistants	YASMINE BRITO
	MIKE CECCONI
	LALIDA SUJJAVASIN
	MIKE TSUCALAS
	STEVEN "BIG PRETTY" RAU
Location Manager	JAMES GIERMAN
Key Assistant Locations Manager	CASSANDRA HEREDIA

Art Department Coordinator	NOREEN COYNE
Art Department Assistant	RUSTIE BURRIS
Leadman	JUSTIN FISHER
On Set Dresser	NINA ALEXANDER
Swing Gang	BRENDAN MAZE
	CHRIS BEAMS
	BRANDON JAY
	HEATHER HAZELWOOD
Post Production Supervisor	LESLIE RODIER
First Assistant Editor	ELLIOT GREENBERG
Post Production Assistants	DONALD ERFERT
	MIKE CECCONI

Visual Effects by
V-DOME

Visual Effects Supervisor/Producer	JOSEPH GROSSBERG
Matte Painting Supervisor	KELVIN McILWAIN

Post production sound services provided by
Skywalker Sound, a Lucasfilm Ltd. Company,
Marin County, California

Re-Recording Mixers	GARY A. RIZZO
	TOM MYERS
Sound Designer	TOM MYERS
Supervising Sound/Dialogue Editor	MICHAEL SILVERS
Sound Effects Editors	MAC SMITH
	DAVID ACCORD
Foley Editor	RICH QUINN
Supervising Assistant Editors	COYA ELLIOTT
	MAC SMITH
Foley Artists	JANA VANCE
	DENISE THORPE
	ELLEN HEUER
Foley Mixer	FRANK AGLIERI-RINELLA
Foley Recordist	SEAN ENGLAND
Mix Technicians	JUAN PERALTA
	BRANDON PROCTOR
Digital Transfer	JONATHAN GREBER
	CHRISTOPHER BARRON
	JOHN COUNTRYMAN
Machine Room Operators	BRIAN MAGERKURTH
	RON ROUMANS
Video Services	ED DUNKLEY
	JOHN “JT” TORRIJOS
Engineering Services	ALAN MAYS
	STEVE MORRIS
	CLAYTON WOOD

Digital Editorial Services	DAVID HUNTER
	LEFFERT LEFFERTS
Client Services	MIKE LANE
	EVA PORTER
	RENEE RUSSO
	GORDON NG

Dancers

ANTHONY MARCIONA
CHRISTOPHER MARTINEZ
JASON YRIBAR
MICHAEL HIGGINS
RESHMA GAJJAR
BRYAN ANTHONY
DESI JEVON
KELLY COOPER
MICHELLE ELKIN
TRACY PHILLIPS
HANNAH FELDNER-SHAW
SHAWN BREATHWAITE
AURORAH ALLAIN
DAVEIONE WILLIAMS
KENNY WORMALD
NANCY O'MEARY
CAROLINE RICE
CAREY YSAIS
GORDON HART
KEN BALDWIN
MISHA HAMILTON
JIMMY FEDERICO
JOEL MANNING
RYAN THOMAS
CAROL CONNERS
JASON BEITEL
MARTY KUDELKA
REBECCA LIN
BOBBIE BATES
CHERYL BAXTER
JENNA STEWART
KEVIN WHITAKER
SUSAN CARR GEORGE
KATIE MALIA
SHAWN BREATHWAITE

Construction Coordinator	ERICH SCHULTZ
General Foreman	SCOTT HEAD
Foreman	JESSE BRINGAS
Prop Makers	JEFF SMITH
	GREGG HENDRICKSON
	COREY BURTON
	BRUCE VALDEZ
Lead Set Painters	BRAD MOORHEAD
	BILL CONSTANTINE
Set Painters	JAMES JOYCE
	MICHELLE JOYCE
Sign Writer	FRANK RAMIREZ
Plasterer	NEIL MARRA
Laborers	ANTONIO RAMIREZ
	JOHN DERANIAN
	ELENA LEPE
Studio Teachers	PATTI FOY
	GERRY NEEDLE
	HEATHER FIELDING
Extras Casting	SMITH & WEBSTER/
	DAVIS CASTING
Extras Casting Director	DIXIE DAVIS
Production Video Assist	RAFAEL CASTRO
Unit Publicists	TONY ANGELLOTTI
	NATASHA SUBOVA
Still Photographers	DARREN MICHAELS
	TRACY BENNETT

Transportation Coordinator	DEREK RASER
Transportation Captain	DON FEENEY
Drivers	
JOHN EMBREY	GEOFF TEAGARDIN
DAVID JOSEPH	JAMES VALDES
ERIN MAGIRE	CHUCK THOMASELLO
Catering	ALEX'S GOURMET CATERING
Chef	DENNIS GARCIA
First Assistant Chef	LESTER GARCIA
Second Assistant Chef	ALAN MORK
Craft Service	PHIL SCALISI
Assistant Craft Service	DESIREE MEJIA
Set Medics	JEFF GARDNER
	JAMES WATSON
Construction Medics	ERNIE CASTILLO
	SUZIE VAN DYKE
NEW JERSEY UNIT	
Production Supervisor	ALYSON LATZ
Production Coordinator	SOPHIA LIN
Second Assistant Director	CHRIS CARROLL
Second Second Assistant Director	NICK BELL
Art Director	ELISE VIOLA
Location Manager	IAN McGREGGOR
Accountant	JEN COX
First Assistant Camera	JEB BYERS
Second Assistant Camera	JAMIE FITZPATRICK
Loader	MILLY ITZHAK
Gaffer	JOE QUIRK
Best Boy Electric	MICHAEL GREEN
Electricians	JAMES HARKER
	SATISH SHAHI
Genny Operators	SAADE MUSTAAFA
	MATTHEW FORD
Key Grip	MATT BLADES
Best Boy Grip	PHIL BRADSHAW
Grips	RYAN CALLAHAN
	KIM RIAL
Dolly Grip	KEN McCALLUM
Leadman	CHRIS SYSKO
Boom Operator	PATTIO BROLSMA
Utility Boom	CHRIS FONDULAS
Set Decorator	CHRISTINE WICK
On Set Dresser	JIM WILLIAMS

Set Dressers	TOM GRODY
	MICHAEL GALVIN
	JOHANNA (JOLIE) RUHE
Construction Coordinator	SCOTT ANDERSON
Video Assistant	CHRIS MURPHY
Special Effects	CONRAD BRINK
Transportation Captain	MAURICE FITZGERALD

Drivers

CHRIS COLLINS	DAVID CONELLI
WILLIAM FEATHERSTONE	BOBBY GALLIHER
BRUCE GOLDEN	MICHAEL HOGAN
MICHAEL IRIATE	BOBBY JONES
THOMAS KEARNS	THOMAS MAWYER
THOMAS MORRIS	DOUG WRIGHT
Set Medic	AVERY PAUL
Production Assistants	MARISSA PRICE
	ADAM BUTERA
	JENNIFER COSTURAS
	AMIR KAHN
	VICTORIA MENKE
Craft Service	PATRICIA BARNES

Digital Motion Picture Laboratory Services	LASERPACIFIC, A KODAK COMPANY
Dailies Colorist	BRUCE GOODMAN
Digital Film Recording	LASERPACIFIC, A KODAK COMPANY
Digital Intermediate Services	LASERPACIFIC, A KODAK COMPANY
Digital Timer	DAVE COLE
Color Science	DOUG JAQUA
Digital Data Conform	JEFF CHARLES
	VALANCE EISLEBEN
	STACY UNDERHILL
Digital Film Recording Services	KYLE DEVRIENDT
	DAVID SLAUGHTER
Digital Laboratory Project Managers	ANDRE TREJO
	TRAVIS AVITABILE
	CRAIG BILSKY
Visual Effects Scanning by	PACIFIC TITLE AND ART STUDIO
Head of Scan & Record Operations	MARC ROSS
Imaging Supervisor	BRIAN NOGLE
Dolby Sound Consultant	DAN SPERRY
Optical Soundtrack Negative	NT AUDIO

Legal Counsel Provided by	SLOSS LAW, LLP
	JACKIE ECKHOUSE
	ALISON HUNTER
Rights & Clearances by	HOLLYWOOD SCRIPT RESEARCH
Banking Services Provided by	HSBC BANK
	JANINE HALLOWAY
Payroll Services Provided by	ENTERTAINMENT PARTNERS
Production Insurance Provided by	AON/ALBERT G. RUBIN INSURANCE SERVICES INC.

ADR Recorded at WILSHIRE STAGES
Los Angeles, California

ADR Mixer	ERIC THOMPSON, C.A.S.
ADR Recordist	CHRIS NAVARRO
Mix Engineer	MICHAEL MORONGELL
Mix Facility Coordinator	NEDA JONCICH

Music Score Mixed by	BRIAN DIXON
Assistant to James L. Venable	LORIA ROBERSON
Music Pre-Mix	JENNIFER KES REMINGTON
	NATHANIEL T. CARTIER
	RYAN McCLURE
Digital Recordist	LARRY MAH
Music Mixed at	THE ZEN ROOM
	SCREAMING FAN STUDIOS
Music Editor	ERICH STRATMANN
Music Consultant	JOE RANGEL
Music Clearances	ANGELA LEUS

MUSIC

"(Nothing But) Flowers"
Written by David Byrne,
Christopher Frantz, Jerry Harrison,
Tina Weymouth and Yves N'Djock
Performed by Talking Heads
Licensed Courtesy of EMI Records Ltd.
and Licensed Courtesy of Sire Records
By Arrangement with Warner Music
Group Film and TV Licensing

"Welcome Home"
Written by Kim Bendix Petersen
Performed by King Diamond
Courtesy of Roadrunner Records, Inc.

"The Invisible Guests"
Written by Kim Bendix Petersen
Performed by Jason Mewes and
Jeff Anderson

"Goodbye Horses"
Written by William Garvey
Performed by Q. Lazzarus
Courtesy of MGM Music
Under License from Columbia
Pictures Industries, Inc.

"Smile, I Think She Likes You"
Written and Performed
by James L. Venable
Performed by Quinn Johnson
and James L. Venable
Courtesy of Screaming Fan Records

"An Evening in Paradise"
Written by James L. Venable
Performed by Quinn Johnson, James L.
Venable and Jennifer Kes Remington
Courtesy of Screaming Fan Records

"Raindrops Keep Fallin' On My Head"
Written by Burt Bacharach and Hal David
Performed by B.J. Thomas
Courtesy of Gusto Records, Inc.

"ABC"
Written by Alphonso Mizell,
Freddie Perren, Deke Richards
and Berry Gordy, Jr.
Performed by The Jackson 5
Courtesy of Motown Records
Under License from Universal Music
Enterprises

"1979"
Written by William Corgan
Performed by The Smashing Pumpkins
Courtesy of Virgin Records
Under License from EMI Film and
Television Music

"Naughty Girls (Need Love Too)"
Written by Full Force
Performed by Samantha Fox
Courtesy of Jive Records
By Arrangement with Sony BMG Music
Entertainment

"Everything"
Written and Performed by
Alanis Morissette
Courtesy of Maverick
Recording Company
By Arrangement with Warner Music
Group Film and TV Licensing

"Misery"
Written by David Pirner
Performed by Soul Asylum
Courtesy of Columbia Records
By Arrangement with Sony BMG Music
Entertainment

Executives in Charge of Physical Production	TIMOTHY CLAWSON TRACY MCGRATH
Executive in Charge of Post Production	MICHAEL A. JACKMAN
Executive in Charge of Music	RACHEL LEVY

Special Thanks

Joseph Azzolina, Jr.

Brevent Park & Leonardo Fire Company

The City of Buena Park

The Days Inn, Buena Park

Food Circus Supermarkets, Inc.

Middletown Township

Molly Pitcher Inn

Juana Benavides

Paintings / Posters by Chris Woods courtesy of
www.DianeFarrisGallery.com

Red Bull

The Thapars

UFCW Local 324 (Orange County)

Greg Halibozek & Greg Conger

Weird, NJ

Los Angeles Police Historical Society, Inc.

The director would like to thank:

God – He who keeps my heart beating, and makes me appreciative, and scared.
Jenny – She who keeps my heart beating, and makes me appreciative and scared.
And loved; always loved.
Scott – My true hetero life-mate and second-to-one soul-mate.
Dave – Welcome back, sir. No flicks without you, ever again. Promise.
Jeff – For not only coming back, but for knocking it out of the park and keeping me honest.
Brian – For being the world's best straight man.
Jay – For cleaning up and being the official "Clerks II" spirit bunny.
Rosario – For saying yes and turning in a performance so great, it made me actually believe that Becky would fuck Dante.
Trevor – For an Elias you could pity and love.
Zack and Joey – For the hours of awesome "Train Wreck".
Ming – For being my Lord of the Web-Rings.
Harvey and Bob – For the cash, the green light, and the freedom.
Michael and Marty – For being Lords of the Dance.
Tony – For keeping us on schedule.
Mom and Dad – For years of support and for having sex.
Gail and Byron – For quietly having sex, and for keeping my life running smoothly.
Harley – For being the spring in Dad's step.
Laura – For holding it all together so amazingly.
Ratface – For my favorite set of all time.
Purcell – For his brilliant art.
James – For the perfect location.
Banker – For keeping the axis straight, yet again.
Jason, Ben and Ethan – For making the time.
Wanda and Earthquake – For making the jokes.
Razer X – Wait a second... thank ME, bitch, for rarely having to move a truck this time.

Whit – For crystal clear dirty dialogue.
Gary, Tom and Erich – For Skywalking said dirty dialogue.
Phil and Sloss – For keeping me in the green.
Angellotti – For the ink.
Carol – For keeping all that green straight.
Janda – For the tech and the fandom.
Jon Gordon – For getting the ball rolling before he bolted.
Carla – For taking over from Jon and being easier to look at in the process.
Elliot – For hours of loading.
Darren – For keeping me pic-rich.
Bry – For being the OG Randal.
Walt – For my love of King Diamond.
The Thapars – For letting us back into Quick Stop one more time.
Chappy – For all that cool-ass merch.
Venable – For all that cool-ass score.
Leslie – For a smooth post.
Gooseberg – For burning down Quick Stop.
The Cast – For elevating, not executing.
The Crew – For being the best bunch of artists I've ever worked with.
Maslin – For being as good a friend as she was a critic.
Hawk – For the notes and the history.
Smalls – For taking off the shades once in awhile.
Mattt – For the truth.
NewsAskew.com – For keeping me abreast of what's going on in my life.
The Folks Who Post at www.viewaskew.com - For being a wonderful, mass sounding board.
"The Snowball Effect" – For reminding me how much "Clerks" meant to me.

And "Jersey Girl" – For taking it so hard in the ass and never complaining.

When in downtown Red Bank, New Jersey, or in downtown Westwood, Los Angeles, visit JAY AND SILENT BOB'S SECRET STASH – the two best comic book stores with that name in the entire known universe.

While at JAY AND SILENT BOB'S SECRET STASH, drop tons of coin on fine merchandise manufactured by Graphitti Designs (also, grab a "Sin City" figure while you're at it, because we over-ordered on them).

Wanna know how Dante and Randal got their job at Mooby's? Check out the "Tales from the Clerks" graphic novel, featuring the "Clerks" and "Clerks II" bridge story "Where's the Beef?"

Are you a total shut-in? You don't even have to leave your house to buy my shit. Get out your credit card and visit www.jayandsilentbob.com for a plethora of autographed "Clerks II" crap.

Watch hours and hours of shorts about the making of "Clerks II" at www.clerks2.com.

How's my driving? Let me know at
www.viewaskew.com
www.myspace.com/therealkevinsmith
www.silentbobspeaks.com
www.quickstopentertainment.com

Christ, I spend too much time on the internet...

American Humane Association monitored the animal action.
No animal was harmed in the making of this film

Camera cranes, dollies and remote camera systems by
Chapman/Leonard Studio Equipment, Inc.

Filmed with remote cranes and heads from
Panavision Remote Systems

Dolby Digital In Selected Theatres	SDDS ™ In Selected Theaters	INTERNATIONAL Digital Sound DTS ™ In Selected Theatres
Lighting Equipment Supplied by CINELEASE	Camera OTTO NEMENZ	Technicolor

The persons and events in this motion picture are fictitious.
Any similarity to actual persons or events is unintentional.

This motion picture is protected under laws of the United States and other countries. Unauthorized duplication, distribution or exhibition may result in civil liability and criminal prosecution.

Jay and Silent Bob might return one day.
For now, they're taking it easy.

Goodbye, Horses.

STOP